An Angel Changed My Life

Uplifting true-life stories of miraculous healing

Theresa Cheung

POCKET
BOOKS

LONDON • SYDNEY • NEW YORK • TORONTO

First published in Great Britain by Simon & Schuster UK Ltd, 2010
A CBS Company

Copyright © 2010 by Theresa Cheung

1 3 5 7 9 10 8 6 4 2

Simon & Schuster UK Ltd
1st Floor
222 Gray's Inn Road
London WC1X 8HB

www.simonandschuster.co.uk

Simon & Schuster Australia
Sydney

A CIP catalogue record for this book is available
from the British Library.

ISBN: 978-1-84983-011-9

Typeset by Hewer Text UK Ltd, Edinburgh
Printed and Bound in Great Britain by
CPI Cox & Wyman, Reading RG1 8EX

Contents

Acknowledgements

Writing a book like this can take over your life and there are many people I want to thank. I am indebted to my incredible agent, Clare Hulton, for believing in and making this book happen; my amazing editor, Kerri Sharp, for her sharp insight and encouragement, and everyone at Simon and Schuster for being so very helpful throughout the entire process of writing this book and getting it ready for publication.

I'd also like to take this opportunity to sincerely thank everyone who has written to me over the years to share their inspiring angel stories, or to offer their personal thoughts and insights. I'm deeply grateful to you all because your stories are the heart and soul of this book and I have no doubt that your words will bring hope and comfort to all those who read them.

Special thanks to Ray, Robert and Ruthie for their love and patience while I went into exile to complete this project. And last, but by no means least, special thanks to everyone who reads this book. May it open your mind to the infinite and wonderful possibilities that your angels can offer you through the medium of change, and your heart to the wonder that exists within and around you!

New Beginnings

The truth is that our finest moments are most likely to occur when we are feeling deeply uncomfortable, unhappy, or unfulfilled. For it is only in such moments, propelled by our discomfort, that we are likely to step out of our ruts and start searching for different ways or truer answers.

M. Scott Peck

Some plants grow quickly, some slowly, but the real miracle is that they grow. Within our growing is a miracle, too.

Karen Goldman

Life as we know it is passing away and something new is arising to take its place.

Author unknown

Introduction:
The Miracle of Change

We cannot fully understand this life, until we catch a glimpse of what lies beyond.

Raymond Moody

Yes, I believe in angels. I believe each one of us has a guardian angel who watches over us in this life and the next. I believe that angels can speak through our dreams or our intuition, or through the spirits of loved ones who have passed to the other side. I believe they can reach out to us through coincidences or other signs that have personal meaning for us. And sometimes they can appear in the guise of other people or animals, consciously or unconsciously guided by those from an invisible dimension.

I'm guessing, as you've picked up this book, that either you believe in angels — because you have personal experience of them and are in tune with the message of love and healing they bring — or you are curious about them and want to know more. If it's the latter, I'm not going to try to convince you or offer 'proof' of their reality. I'm hoping, though, that what you read here will at the very least open your mind to the possibility that they are real.

In my opinion, an open mind is the greatest virtue. An open mind can lead to new perspectives and with new perspectives comes the possibility of transformation. An open mind can lift the veil between this world and the world of spirit, where time does not exist and life does not end with death. Without an open mind a person's heart would never be able to change. And without change a person's life would stagnate. There would be no learning, no movement, no experience and no growth.

I've been gathering together collections of real-life angel encounters for close to twenty-five years now from people of all ages, cultures and backgrounds. All these stories differ widely in the details and circumstances, but there are also a number of familiar themes, and one that I've noticed time and time again is the theme of positive change. It seems that whenever and however celestial beings manifest themselves on earth, lives are transformed and changed for ever as a result of the experience. It also seems that change, even the most difficult and painful, is a powerful medium used by angels to reveal themselves to us, and to offer us their gift of spiritual transformation.

Angel stories themselves can also be messengers of change. This is because whenever life-affirming angel stories are shared they have the power to open the minds and hearts of those who read or hear them, even if these people have not seen beings of light themselves. They have this transformative power because they are a reminder that there is goodness and love in the world and that miracles really can and do happen.

In my own life it took me quite a while to realize what a truly beautiful gift from my angels change can be. Like many people, I resisted it at every opportunity because I was frightened of the 'devil' I didn't know. Looking back, I can see now that it wasn't until I was able to embrace change, face up to my fears and step out from the comfort of the familiar that my spiritual journey could truly begin.

Running away

Fifteen years ago I was thirty years old. I should have felt happy and fulfilled. I had just married the most amazing man and my writing career was beginning to blossom. Not only that but I was making slow but gradual progress with my psychic development. I couldn't 'see' or 'hear' my angels yet, and it was a source of huge disappointment to me that I hadn't sensed the presence of my mother in spirit, but comforting dreams and coincidences were giving me inspiration, strength and hope. With years of loneliness, hard times and struggle behind me, and so much happiness to look forward to, I should have felt on top of the world. But I didn't. On the outside I was all smiles, but inside there was still an emptiness; an emptiness that wouldn't go away.

I did not realize it at the time, but instead of dealing with these feelings of emptiness I tried to escape them, by quite literally running away. Ever since my teens I had been an active and health-conscious person. Eating healthily and exercising regularly were an important part of my life. I especially loved to run.

I'd always been an energetic person. At school I used to find it hard to sit still in lessons; I would dream of running away.

With so much energy to burn, I was naturally drawn to sport and movement of all kinds. My first love was dancing. I must have been fairly good because when I was sixteen, I was offered no less than four scholarships from dance academies in London. Trouble was, the scholarships only paid the tuition fees. My poor mother just didn't have the money to pay the living, clothing and accommodation expenses required so my dancing dreams ended almost as soon as they began. Bitterly disappointed, I refocused my efforts on getting into university, but this only used up my mental energy. I needed an outlet for my physical energy. Being a bit shy, I found it in running.

I can't remember when running switched from being something I enjoyed to being a compulsion, but I think it was probably a series of events that all led to this. During the height of my dancing years, when I still believed a career might be possible and I wanted my body to look perfect, I had a brush with anorexia and running certainly played a part in keeping my calorie intake down. Fortunately, I did manage to overcome anorexia and reach a healthy weight in my late teens, but even though I was eating enough, I continued to exercise at an intense level. I convinced myself and everyone else that it was a healthy habit, because I looked and felt fit and was not underweight.

At university, I felt insecure and out of place, and the only thing that made me feel strong and confident was running, so my schedule increased. When I left university and entered the world of work, and went through a series of disastrous relationships, running became the only constant factor in my life. And then when my mum died, and my heart crumbled and I felt more lost and alone than ever before, running became the central focus of my life.

I met my future husband at a gym, because he also loved to keep fit. It was an interest, a passion we shared, which was a good thing, but I don't think he realized how addicted I was to exercise until after the wedding. On our honeymoon the first signs of tension appeared when I was simply unable to give myself a rest day from my running. There we were in the stunningly gorgeous Hawaii. We should have been enjoying every precious moment together, creating happy memories for years to come. Instead, there was I running alone at five a.m. along the beach, and there was my husband asleep by himself in the hotel room. I would come back at seven a.m., take a shower and creep quietly back into bed.

One morning I overslept. I woke up at seven a.m. without having done my run. I think the sense of panic got to me and I started to cry and cry. Even on days when I did get my run in early, there were moments when for no reason at all I would get this urge to put on my running shoes. I would be looking at a beautiful sunset, or walking along the beach, but I couldn't enjoy it. I had to run some more.

Things went from bad to worse once we got home from our honeymoon. My husband, as may be fairly typical for some men when they get married, gradually lost interest in working out. He wanted to go to restaurants, the movies or the theatre or for walks in the park instead. He was enjoying married life. How I wished I could too. I went to restaurants, parks and the movies with him, but all the time in my head I was calculating when my next workout would be. I had this target of running for at least two hours a day, and sometimes when my husband was working abroad this target would stretch to four hours a day.

I did not realize it, and few would have guessed it because my chosen addiction was a so-called 'healthy' one, but I was living the lifestyle of an addict. I was dependent on exercise to make me feel good. Deep down, though, I was trying to fill an inner void. I was trying to escape anxiety.

About four months into my marriage I was finding it harder and harder to enjoy any aspect of my life. Whether or not it was a good day or a bad day depended on how much I had exercised. It was putting my marriage under strain and I knew I had to do something, but I felt powerless.

And then I met an angel, and that angel changed my life.

It was a warm sunny morning and I was doing my usual early-bird run. I must have been going for about thirty minutes when I passed this lady sitting on a bench. I remember her clearly because she was looking at me and smiling. I tried but failed to smile back. On my route back she was sitting there still, but this time she had been joined by another woman. I noticed that they were both wearing blue coats and they looked exactly alike, so I guessed they must have been twins.

As I passed the bench, my left shoelace suddenly came undone. Hastily, I bent down to do it up and while I was fumbling around I heard one of the women talk quietly under her breath to the other. I can't remember the exact words but it was something along the lines of, 'Let's hope the lace doesn't do up, so she has to walk. You know, I see her out every day running and she always looks so miserable. She doesn't seem to enjoy it at all.'

The woman's words made me angry. I stood up, flashed a beaming, toothy grin at her to prove I was enjoying myself and ran home. All day long I kept recalling what she had said and it made me feel tense and uptight.

The next morning I set off again on my usual route. Thankfully, the bench was empty this time, but on the way back I noticed a man sitting there. Incredibly, my laces came undone again at almost exactly the same spot, but this time I didn't realize fast enough and I fell over right in front of the bench. The man immediately got up to help me to my feet and asked me if I was OK. I was a bit shaken so I sat down beside him for a while to gather myself.

When I'd been sitting for a few moments the man started to talk to me. He told me that he loved getting up early to watch the world wake up and he had often seen me run. He told me he admired my discipline and for some reason I can't explain – perhaps I was feeling sorry for myself – I told him that not everyone felt the same, especially the ladies in the blue coats sitting on the bench together yesterday. The man gave me the strangest look and he wiped away a tear as he told me his wife had passed away three years ago in a car accident with her twin sister. They had both been wearing identical blue coats at the time. The bench we were sitting on was one he had put up in their honour. He thanked me with all of his heart for telling him this. It meant the world to him and it was the sign he had been longing and praying for. It gave him great comfort to think of her sitting there, taking in the view and commenting on the world passing by, as she always used to with her beloved sister.

For the first time in years that day instead of running I walked home. There was so much to mull over in my head and I needed the silence and the peace of walking. It could, of course, have all been a coincidence, but what a coincidence! My laces getting undone at exactly the same place for two days in a row; two women looking very much like twins, sitting on that bench in identical coats; a bench dedicated to twin sisters who had died together.

My mind and heart raced. There was a very strong and real possibility that I had experienced something supernatural. It was an awesome and humbling thought. Then my mind turned to what the woman had actually said about me. Whether she had been human or divine her words were sobering. She had said I didn't look very happy, and she had been right. What was I really running away from?

In that instant, as I walked home and listened to the birds singing, I realized something that had been plainly obvious to everyone but me all these years: running wasn't making me happy. It wasn't ever going to make me happy. It was simply distracting me from feelings of emptiness inside. And the reason I felt empty inside was that I wasn't fulfilled emotionally and spiritually. There was still a little child inside me crying out in pain, asking to be loved and feeling unlovable. I had needed the running to numb how I was feeling about myself so I could function in the world. It was time now to stop running away and take responsibility for my own inner healing.

My mum had often told me happiness can't be found on the outside, only on the inside, but until that day I had never really got it. I had been searching for it in all the wrong places. That lady on the bench, whoever she was, had helped me see that Mum had been right all along. I had to find stillness within and connect with the higher, spiritual part of myself, because only with that sense of inner fulfilment could I break free from depression and addictive, compulsive behaviour and find lasting happiness and peace. I also had to understand that it was impossible to avoid anxiety. To live a fulfilling life, we have to face our fears – make mistakes, be wrong, be laughed at, be criticised, be average – and we have to learn to deal with our anxieties. Behind my addictive behaviour was the fantasy that being perfect, or the best, would end my anxiety, but as long as I am human perfection is impossible. I had to realize and accept that good enough *is* good enough. Only then could I free myself to live the life of my dreams and enjoy the journey.

From that moment on I gradually began to shut down my running schedule and open my mind and heart to the magic and wonder of my life. It wasn't always easy, but after meeting my guardian angel – as I like to call her – on a bench I started to replace my pain with feelings of self-acceptance and, dare I say it, self-love. And the more I was able to do that the more my confidence grew and the more the veil between this life and the world of spirit gradually started to lift. It would take me a few more years to fully appreciate what happened – and what I am writing here I freely admit is with the gift of hindsight – but I now wholeheartedly believe that my guardian angel spoke to me and changed my life that day.

I went on to have several more angel experiences, all of which changed my life in incredible ways, and as my life transformed I made it my mission to collect together in book form other remarkable stories from people whose lives have likewise been dramatically changed, healed or saved by angels. Many of these awesome stories you'll find gathered together here for you in this book.

Magic moments

In everyone's life, there are moments when the wind shifts direction and life changes for ever. My 'angel on a bench' story fifteen years ago was one of those moments; moments when life is forever changed. Days, months and years after these moments pass you can look back on them and remember them with absolute clarity. They seem so real and so alive. They are infused with a potent mixture of insight, feelings and perception. In these instants, you fly above the routines of your daily life and in a wonderful 'eureka' moment glimpse the bigger picture. You feel free and at home at last, with a wellspring of compassion, understanding, acceptance and love not just for yourself but for all living things. Everything that has happened in your life makes perfect sense. For the briefest of moments you know, without any need for explanation, that there is a divine purpose to your life and angels are always watching over you.

There are countless different ways in which people's lives can change completely in a single moment. For some, life is a series of gentle, gradual progressions. For others, it seems to move from one crisis to the next. And for others it appears to float along in a simple, almost predestined way. But no matter how smooth or dramatic a person's life appears to be on the outside, there is always some moment along the way which turns everything on its head, and nothing is ever the same again.

This book is about these moments: instants when lives are transformed and miraculously changed for ever. It will show you that it is in these divine moments that your angels are reaching out to you as never before. It will show you that it is through the medium of change, even changes that hurt and are hard to cope with or accept, that your angels offer you the opportunity to become more than you ever thought you could be.

Angel visions

Since that 'lady on a bench' moment all those years ago an ever-increasing flow of remarkable angel stories has been coming my way, stories that have these fundamentals – an unexpected moment of revelation or deep recognition, an experience of time and place suspended, and, very often, an awakening of hopes and unsung dreams that changes everything in a person's life for the better.

I can say with absolute certainty that each one of us has had or will have a life-changing moment or even a series of life-changing moments. It comes with being human. Few of us realize, though, that in these moments our angels have never been closer and if we open our hearts and minds to them we can begin to see them all around and within us. And once we begin to see them our lives won't just change, they will transform.

I'm often asked what angel visions are and my answer is that they are a glimpse of heaven on earth. The form may be anything. Some people actually see angels complete with wings and halos. Some may hear a voice out of nowhere, or encounter the spirit of a departed loved one, but such dramatic encounters are rare. You are far more likely to encounter angels in subtler, but no less powerful ways, such as a stunning coincidence, a sign that has profound meaning to you or in a flash of intuition or a meaningful dream. They may manifest as a gentle breeze, a cloud, a bird, a coin, a song, the actions of a stranger or anything that speaks volumes to your heart and reminds you of the love and goodness in ourselves.

All the stories you'll find here are told by ordinary but extraordinary people. All of them are convinced that angels dipped into their lives and changed everything for the better. It wasn't hard at all for me to collect these stories together. Since the publication of my first angel books, they have literally flown in my direction, proving to me that supernatural experiences are happening all around us, all the time, and ordinary people of all ages and from all walks of life, in all corners of the world, are being touched by something that is giving them remarkable courage, hope and inspiration.

In my work as an angel writer over the years it is has become clear to me that angels are becoming real to and changing the lives of growing numbers of people today, and the reality of the message of hope, healing and love they bring is making people feel happy and safe again. I believe that right now, here in the present day as never before, it is a time for angels.

A time for angels

The speed of change today is far faster than it has ever been. For many of us it is increasingly tough to know how to handle it all. Relationships begin and end quickly, careers change in a heartbeat, news flashes up on laptops changing or altering our opinions and perceptions, not to mention the fact that religion, the glue that used to unite people, is now dividing them.

Amid all this rapid change, it is not hard to see that things have gone very wrong today. Despite massive scientific and techno-logical advances, inhumanity has not been eradicated. Images of injustice, violence, poverty and cruelty are everywhere. The world itself is showing signs of 'disease' with pollution and climate extremes. We even have the potential to destroy our beautiful world with nuclear weapons. The whole planet appears to be dramatically altered, and what was meaningful for us centuries ago has paled into insignificance when compared to our scientific and technological advances. Things we used to think of as sacred and unchanging are no longer so.

It's no wonder we feel so displaced. Our material world is changing so fast it largely ignores our spiritual needs. It's not that our lives and relationships and careers today lack integrity or purpose, or that there is anything wrong with progress – it goes much deeper than that. There is a sense that the things society today puts value on – wealth, power, status, celebrity – can't truly bring us the hope, inspiration and fulfilment we crave. We feel a loss of meaning. It's like homesickness, a longing for something more, even though we don't really know what that 'something more' is.

There's no doubt we live in a time of rapid and often confusing change, but I hope what you read here will show you that every change, whether big or small, personal or global, can, with the guidance of your angels, also be an opportunity for spiritual growth and transformation. And this is why our angels are here, right now. This is why they have chosen this moment in time to reveal themselves as never before. They are here because we each need a spiritual lift – a huge one – to wake us up to the possibilities offered by all these rapid changes, rather than the conflicts, stresses, confusion, suffering and tensions that are all too often created by them.

We all need to be reminded of the eternal things that don't change during times of great change. We all need to remember that the wonders of the external world are nothing compared to the wonders of the invisible world of spirit. We all need to reconnect with our angels. We all need miracles to feel centred and secure again. We all need our faith restored in ourselves, in each other and in the power of eternal love to transcend suffering, conflict, injustice and even death itself.

And that is why, perhaps more than ever before in human history, this is the moment for miracles and divine intervention. This is the time to embrace rather than fear change, leave our limitations behind and become all we are capable of becoming, so that we ourselves can become agents of the miraculous. This is the time for us to listen to the angels within and around us and turn the destructive course of the human race around.

Yes, this is a time of rapid and confusing change, but it is also a time for angels.

About this book

The time has also never felt so right for this book to be published. This wasn't always the case, though. In keeping with the theme of change, there has been a huge shift in recent years in attitudes towards the supernatural. As I write this introduction, my previous angel title – *An Angel Healed Me* – has been in the *Sunday Times* top-10 non-fiction paperback bestsellers for three weeks, rising as high as number 4 at one point. This alone shows just how many people out there are in tune with the message of hope and healing angels bring.

Fifteen years ago when I first started writing books this would never have been possible. For a start, mainstream publishers would have been reluctant to take on such a book, and if it was published the readership would not have been there or it would have been greeted with scepticism and derision. However, for a number of reasons, which include the decline of religion, and the rise of the internet – where angel experiences have become a uniting rather than a dividing force between people of all races, religions and backgrounds – angels are now without doubt a prominent spiritual movement. In addition to countless websites devoted to them, there are numerous angel books, newsletters, magazines and so on, as well as angel collectables and memorabilia.

In a word, angels are everywhere and, as mentioned above, with pain and suffering in the world spiralling out of control, there can be no better time for the growing angel movement to manifest itself, or for this book to appear to add its voice to the message and the movement. We urgently need to be reminded that there is love, goodness and hope in the world and that it is more than a match for hatred, pain and hopelessness. And I sincerely hope, as you read this book, that you will be reminded that however difficult your life gets, however many changes of direction there are, your very own guardian angel is always by your side – a constant, loving presence who wants to help and guide you. All you need to do is open your mind and heart to the reality that you are never alone and that in this life and the next your angels will be always be there to lift your spirit and give you wings.

I also hope this book will encourage you to look at every change you have to face in your life as an opportunity to grow, instead of something to dread. When I was finally able to relax and embrace the opportunity of change, things started to fall into place in my life. I didn't find life such a struggle any more. I didn't have to chase the writing career I longed for; it found me. I didn't have to chase angels; they found me. And nothing illustrates this better than the fact that I am writing this book.

Most people can't believe that I'm not a celebrity and my books aren't about crime, horror and misery, but I've somehow had book after bestselling book published. How can books by an unknown author about miracles, love, hope and healing, and not the typical trend for misery memoirs or celebrity tell-all, fly off the shelves? They say I must be very lucky to be writing about what inspires me. I have great delight in replying that my life hasn't been easy. I grew up in disadvantage and there have been many struggles along the way. The reason for my success now is that I have finally learned to listen to my angels and hear what they are saying to me. There isn't a day that goes by when I don't thank them for their guidance.

Another reason I believe my angel-story collections are gaining a readership of their own is that people are being guided to them. I've had so many letters from people telling me that they went into a bookshop or library without intending to buy or borrow an angel book, but somehow felt drawn to it. Or they tell me that a kind friend or loved one has sent it to them as a surprise gift, or they just saw it in a friend's house, or they noticed someone reading it on the Tube and were intrigued, or in several cases they were lent a copy by a doctor or someone sharing a hospital ward. I have great faith that the book will somehow appear in the hands of those who are meant to read it. I have this faith because this book was written from the heart – the place where angels emerge – and through the stories of ordinary people whose lives have been touched by the extraordinary, it will reach out and speak to the hearts of those destined to read it.

Before getting going with these astonishing true-life stories, in the first chapter of this book I want to continue the journey

I began in my previous angel books – the journey of my own spiritual and psychic development. I feel it is important for my readers to get a sense of who I am and where I came from. I also feel that in order to appreciate and interpret the stories of other people, it is important for me not only to have had similar experiences but also to understand them.

However, just because extraordinary things have happened to me in my life, and I hope they will continue to do so as nothing gives me more joy, I don't want you to think that I'm some kind of 'angel lady' or 'psychic' or 'medium' or someone with the so-called 'gift'. I'm nothing of the sort. I'm an ordinary forty-something mum of two (my son is twelve and my daughter is ten) with no greater psychic ability than the average person in the street. I may have been born into a family of psychics and spiritualists but I didn't inherit the gift. In fact, it wasn't until my late thirties that my spiritual journey really began. Until then, I tried so hard to see angels but the harder I tried the further away they seemed. And when my breakthrough moment of awareness finally came it wasn't through blinding lights and visions, but through the subtle, gentle language of dreams, coincidences and signs. This has led me to believe that every one of us is born with the ability to see angels. And even though pessimism and fear can shut down our connection with heaven as we get older, and make us resistant to change and spiritual growth, we can all find ways to cut through the darkness and rediscover the love of our angels and the magical potential for spiritual transformation inside and all around us. Indeed, you don't need any special gifts at all to see angels. All you need is an open mind and an open, trusting heart.

Following the first chapter outlining some of my spiritual journey, so that you can see that anyone, whatever their age or background, can transform their life with the help of the angels, the remaining chapters of the book form the core of this book because in them I explore some of the astonishing 'angel stories' I have encountered over the years. As always I am deeply grateful to all the people who gave me permission to share their experiences and their integrity. A few sent in their own versions of their experiences, but in most cases I have written up the stories from what I have been told or sent. It's a privilege and an honour for me to share these deeply personal experiences with a wider audience and if your story isn't here, please forgive me, it is simply because time and space would not allow me . . . this time.

True accounts

Along with the theme of change, another connecting feature of this book, and all my writing, is that the stories, to the best of my knowledge, are true. They actually happened to the people who sent them. I have no reason to doubt the integrity of my contributors, who are ordinary people with ordinary lives, jobs and opinions.

Although some of my contributors already believed in angels, just as many did not until their experience. Some were religious, but others were not. Like more and more people these days, they believed in something but were not sure what. And then there were those who did not believe in anything at all until an angel changed their lives.

Many of the people who contributed to this book were hugely relieved to tell me their stories, sometimes for the first time. They wanted them included not for personal glory – as in most cases names and personal details have been changed to protect identity – but because they hoped that sharing their stories would be a source of comfort, healing and inspiration to others, especially to those facing periods of crisis, turmoil, trauma or grief. They wanted others to know that angels are always with us, even when we don't think we can see or hear them. At the end of the day, all the true stories are accounts that bring a simple message of support, hope and love through angel encounters that transform this life and offer tantalizing glimpses of the next.

Save a seat for your angel

When I was a very young girl, my great-aunt Rose – who was a much-respected spiritualist and medium in her day – always used to tell me whenever I sat down to save a part of my seat for my guardian angel. It still makes me smile now to think of myself shuffling forward in my seat without hesitation or doubt to make way for my invisible guest. I'm not asking you to save a part of your seat at this point, but I would like you to save a place in your heart for your guardian angel and prepare to be inspired and astonished – as I never fail to be – by the incredible stories of people leading outwardly normal lives, but who have been healed, saved and transformed by heavenly beings.

Some of the stories you will read here may take your breath away. Some will move you, or even stretch your belief. Some might remind you of experiences you may have had. The mind often forgets what it struggles to explain. As you read this book you may even be able to look back at your own life and remember, perhaps for the first time, life-changing moments you have experienced and finally recognize them as angelic in origin.

Working on this book has once again renewed my connection to the realm of spirit and, as you'll see in the next chapter, helped me dip into my life and draw incredible comfort from the knowledge that even though I thought my angels weren't with me, they were there all along. I just didn't know how to recognize them. It is my sincere wish when you read it that it will serve as a catalyst for your own belief by proving to you that angels are real, and even ordinary people, like you and me, can wake up one day and encounter an angel who changes our life for ever.

Who are they?

There is, of course, often no proof for an angel encounter, just the word of the person who has experienced it. In our rational world that expects scientific proof of angels, this can be a source of frustration and disbelief for many, even though in a court of law a witness statement is taken as evidence. Also, just because there is no proof for something, or we can't actually see it ourselves, does not mean it does not exist. Take love, for example – we all know it to be real, even though we can't actually see it. Science itself is also discovering many things it cannot prove, but believes to be true – ephemeral matter, curved space, liquid time, to name but a few – and there is no reason why angel encounters should be regarded as any different. Indeed, from a quantum-scientific perspective, angel encounters are simply things that humans have yet to understand well enough.

But who are these celestial beings, these beings of light, and these forces of goodness bringing glimpses of heaven to earth? Like trying to prove the existence of angels, trying to explain who or what they are is equally impossible because by definition miracles are unexplainable, just as, by definition, faith is to believe without proof. At the end of the day it all comes down to belief and to those who believe in angels there is no need for proof or explanation. Nothing will ever have the power of their heartfelt trust.

The power and love of your angels is boundless and perhaps it is best to consider every angel story as a gift that should be received with gratitude and humility, rather than a mystery that should be solved. Perhaps it is wisest to just keep an open mind and let the stories and the angels you read about here speak for themselves, let them work their magic on your life, as they did in the lives of the people who experienced them.

Perhaps when you finish this book you will be able to decide for yourself, or perhaps you will not make your mind up at all. Your heart may be touched by the stories, or you may forget them . . . but whatever impact the stories have on you, the work of this book is done because deep down a part of you will know that once an angel dips into your life, it will never be the same again. And one day when the time is right for you, this hidden 'knowing' may emerge from your heart, and when it does your life will change for ever, because you will know that you are never alone. You will know, without any doubt or fear, that your guardian angel is always right beside you.

Your Guardian Angel

You have a Guardian Angel
Who watches over you —
Everywhere you go
And everything you do.

This gentle, silent helper
Is there to be your guide
To shelter and protect you,
And for you to walk beside.

Your Angel will always help you
Whenever things go wrong,
They'll be the wings beneath your feet
As Life's path you walk along.

Feel this calming presence —
Be enfolded by its love
And let your life be guided
By a power from above.

Unknown

CHAPTER 1

An Angel Changed My World

On earth, an angel's wings are inside.

Karen Goldman

'Please don't leave me. Please,' I shouted through the letterbox of my boyfriend's flat, or should I say ex-boyfriend.

The past few days had been a blur of desperation, pain and anguish for me. My boyfriend didn't want to be with me any more but I needed to be with him. Being apart hurt so much. And that's why on a cold, November morning, I found myself sitting outside his flat crying, pleading for him to open the door. Just two weeks previously we had been talking about going on holiday together. How could his feelings for me have changed so dramatically from one week to the next? If only he would see me, I was sure he would change his mind. Perhaps he was testing me, to see just how much I loved him.

Twenty-three years ago my then boyfriend walked out of my life, leaving me with intense feelings of pain, guilt, loss, confusion, rejection and anguish. At the time, I wanted to die. He had been my first boyfriend, and in my mind the last. I couldn't understand what I had done wrong. In the two years we'd been together I'd done everything I could to help and support him during bouts of stress and illness. I had always put him first. Now that he was getting better, he was putting me last. I had lived for him and I didn't know how to live without him. I wanted to die.

My ex-boyfriend never answered the door that day. I knew he was in and I knew there was another woman with him, but I was so desperate to see him that I would have forgiven him anything. It hadn't always been that way. When we first met, he was the one who had done all the chasing. I had a busy life and a job I loved. I hadn't even been looking for a boyfriend, but we kept bumping into each other and he kept asking me out, so eventually I said yes.

The first days and months of our relationship were breathless. I'd never been in a serious relationship before. I'd got so used to it being me and Mum, it was amazing to have someone just for me. We spent every moment together. As lovers do, we laughed, we chatted for hours about life, the universe and everything.

I convinced myself that this was it; this was the love of my life. There were moments when doubts crept in. When he didn't want me to see my friends, or go to my dance classes, or do anything without telling him first, I did sometimes wonder if we would go the distance, or if he was right for me, but a part of me liked his possessiveness. It felt good to be wanted. Even though I was a child of the Sixties, I was an old-fashioned girl at heart, with a very traditional view of relationships. He was my man. It was my duty to love and honour and obey him and that was the way it was going to be for the rest of my life.

How wrong I was. A year into our relationship the fact that my boyfriend didn't have a job, and was making it hard for me to keep mine with his constant need for attention, didn't shake my conviction that this was for life. I believed, as I still do, that love is about caring for someone in both the good times and the bad times. It didn't dawn on me that our relationship was all about the bad times and I was the one doing all the giving and he was the one doing all the taking.

My boyfriend was a good ten years older than me, but he still hadn't found a career to devote himself to. He was full of schemes and ideas but that was as far as it got. He always had excuses for why he couldn't get a job or train for something. He told me that he was an artist, but I never saw him paint. He told me he longed to be a poet, but I never read any of his poems. He told me that it was his curse to be undecided in his purpose in life. Increasingly, all our conversations were taken up with his confusions and his complicated relationship with his mother. Rarely rising before one p.m., because he also suffered from chronic fatigue when it suited him, he would cry if I didn't come home from work to make him lunch. He would cry when I left. I felt guilty leaving him and would count the minutes until five p.m. when I could meet him. Then it would be endless talking and coffee-drinking again until the early hours of the morning. Sometimes I would arrive at work with just two or three hours' sleep under my belt.

Needless to say my health and my job suffered. I was given a warning at work when someone reported me for being on the phone to my boyfriend for over an hour in my boss's office one day when she was out on an assignment. He was having one of his panic attacks and I had to calm him down. I didn't last long after the warning and was politely offered voluntary redundancy when the company had a reshuffle. Even though I had loved my job — and excelled in it before I met my boyfriend — I was happy to take the package and throw myself into freelance work. Despite the loneliness and unpredictability of freelance work, I told myself it was the right thing to do, and best of all I would have more time to care for my sick boyfriend.

Caring for my boyfriend didn't just take up more of my time, it took up all of my time and for three months I moved in with him. I became completely attuned to his needs. I lost contact with all my friends, and my opinions. My dreams of freelancing were put on the back burner. I needed to put him first. Once he got better, everything would be better.

A real low point came one night when I fell asleep just before midnight. I was woken up to find my boyfriend red with rage and anger. He told me I was selfish for falling asleep and I didn't love him at all. Still groggy with sleep, I snapped back at him and told him he was selfish keeping me awake because I needed to get to sleep. I was tired. Like a volcano, he erupted and lashed out at me and thumped me so hard in the back I was winded. He said that I was being cruel and thoughtless reminding him how hard it was for him to fall asleep. When I curled into a ball in fear, he hit me again, saying that this would make it easier for me to play the victim.

It was insane. I should have grabbed my bags and run, but I didn't. I stayed with him and I took more and more abuse. I wanted to help him, you see. I wanted him to know that my love was stronger than both of us. I thought my love for him would change him, transform him into the man of my dreams. I lived my life around his every mood and whim. I watched him constantly, trying to assess how I was doing in my role of girlfriend.

My experience with my boyfriend was not the first relationship I had tried to control by being so eager to please, by making myself indispensable. I had behaved in a similar way with my girlfriends, from school age onwards. If they were in a bad mood, I thought it was because I was boring. If they didn't call me for a chat it was because they didn't like me any more. They'd met someone more interesting. If they needed help, or something done, it was my job to do it. If they didn't like the clothes I wore or my haircut, I would change them.

Looking back, I can clearly see now that my identity had become an extension of the person I was with. If my friends didn't have time for me, I felt invisible. If my boyfriend praised me, I mattered. I was constantly afraid that every person I got close to would eventually reject me if I wasn't the perfect match for his or her identity. I was setting myself an impossible task. The harder I tried to win someone's love or friendship, the deeper my feelings of self-doubt and inner conflict became.

Regarding myself as a person worthy of love and friendship, a person who could be valued for who and what they were on their own terms, was beyond my understanding. Although I had had a loving relationship with my mother as I had grown up, with an absent father I had taken responsibility for her needs and feelings at far too young an age. There were serious problems with my self-image.

Returning to that cold and biter day all those years ago, after sitting crying on the doorstep of my boyfriend's flat for several hours, I knew he wasn't going to answer the door. In my desperation I hid behind his dustbin and followed him and his new girlfriend when they finally got up and went out. I watched them hold hands and laugh together as they walked down the street and sat in the same cafe we had spent so many hours in. I watched him push a lock of her hair behind her ear in exactly the same way he used to do for me. It was pure torture following them, but I couldn't tear myself away. I spent the rest of the day hiding in the shadows, lurking around corners watching them. Were there any depths to which I would not sink? I had become little more than a stalker.

Finally, exhaustion took over and I went back home to my mum and shut myself in my room for three days. I had given my all to the relationship, but it hadn't been enough. Being caring and constantly available for others – these were the only ways I knew to create relationships. I was dependent on the approval of others. There had been low points in my life before but perhaps nothing quite as desperate. I was closer to considering dying as a favourable option than at any other time.

I remember one terrifying moment a few weeks after the break-up when I was standing waiting for a Tube train to arrive.

When it rushed into the tunnel a savage longing inside me made me want to jump. All I needed to do to take away the pain was step forward. Time stood still for a moment and then I felt this tap on my shoulder.

I wasn't with anyone, and considered not turning around, but then I felt the tap again. I turned around and saw a little lady smiling at me. She looked about seventy years old. I can't be sure. She may have been elderly but there was something mischievous in her eyes that made her look young. 'You've dropped your handkerchief, love,' she said, pointing to something on the floor. 'I'd bend down and pick it up for you, but my back's been playing up recently. It's a really pretty handkerchief. I think you'll be sorry to lose it.'

I looked down and sure enough, there was my handkerchief. It was indeed a special one as it had been a gift from my grandmother with my initials embroidered on it. I bent down to pick it up and mumbled my thanks before the train arrived and we both stepped inside.

There were only two seats left, so we ended up sitting together. I think the lady must have noticed my red eyes, so she asked me if I was OK. I said I was fine, but it was clear that she didn't believe me. 'Let me guess,' she said. 'It's a fella, isn't it, and you've been crying your eyes out into that pretty handkerchief of yours. I'll tell you what I've always told my daughters and my granddaughters when their hearts got broke: "Don't go crying over someone who isn't going to cry over you."'

The Tube stopped at the next station and the lady got off. As the doors closed, I saw her smile and wave at me. For the first time in weeks I managed to smile feebly back at her. I can't say how or why but something inside me told me she was right. I could feel a subtle energy flow throughout my body. There was also a feeling of calm and peace I had not felt for many weeks. I had this quiet but deep knowledge that this lady, whoever she was, knew about my pain and that I had needed to meet her. Within minutes of seeing her, all thoughts of dying had vanished. We had spoken for only the briefest of moments, but I believe I was destined to meet her.

As I walked down the Tube platform that day it gradually became clear to me that I was crying over someone who had not given the 100 per cent I had to the relationship. I had done all the giving and he had done all the taking. Why was I crying over someone who didn't truly care for me? Why was I wasting my energy on a relationship that had drained me? Surely I should be spending my time on people who were there for me?

You might think that following this profound encounter I would never again have been so gullible and frightened, as far as relationships were concerned. While it is true that the pieces of my life started to come together again, old habits die hard, and a part of me still chased approval from the people I was closest to. I still worried about what they thought. I still wanted to please them.

One year after the break-up, I had thrown my energy into my freelance career as a writer and journalist and my determination and dedication were rewarding me. Unfortunately, though, my lifelong habit of making other people's opinions more important than my own was exacerbated by a job that depended on the approval of others. I was hopelessly addicted to approval. If a job went well and I got positive feedback, I was on a high. If there were problems or rejections, I'd slump.

Often I'd work through the night to hit unrealistic deadlines. Saying 'no' just wasn't in my vocabulary. I wanted to be the one everyone could count on, whatever the cost. Inevitably, long hours and endless demands started to catch up on me. I was simply taking on too much work for one person.

Then one night everything came to a head. I had a nine a.m. deadline the following morning for a series of articles on supernatural events. They were nowhere near ready for sending. I needed to do much more research and interviewing. With a 10,000 word count expected, and several thousand words yet to write, any sensible writer would have known it was an impossible task to complete in one night. But I was going to attempt the impossible. I hit the keyboard and bashed away for hours.

Every time my eyes felt heavy, I fought sleep with caffeine but eventually – it must have been about four a.m. – my head instead of my fingers hit the keyboard and I must have dozed off. What happened then was truly astonishing. I fell into a deep sleep and started to dream. In my dream I was running beside a very fast stream. It was hard to keep up but I managed to do so. Eventually, I came to a bridge and on that bridge I saw a figure. As I came closer, I could see that the figure was a little girl and she looked so familiar. I was sure I knew her. I just didn't know who she was. When I walked onto the bridge it started to rise into the air. The little girl laughed and ran up to me. Holding my hand she told me to trust her. I didn't feel frightened at all and the two of us rose into the air. We were flying. I looked down on the world below and it was so beautiful. The little girl told me that I was very close to a great spiritual awakening and that anyone who wanted a deeper, richer understanding of their purpose in this life and the next needed to go through difficult phases like this. Then she told me that from now on I needed to look to her for good feelings about myself.

When I woke up, for a brief moment I felt a sense of comfort and calm, but then I looked at the screen in front of me and panic set in again. A large portion of text had gone. I must have hit the delete key when I was sleeping on the keyboard. I looked at my watch and it was nine-thirty a.m.. I had already missed my deadline.

My stomach turned and I rushed to the kitchen to get a glass of water. I would have to do what I feared the most: let other people down. After gulping down some water, I sat with my head in my hands and started to cry. It was only then that my dream flashed into my mind. I remembered every detail with perfect clarity, but this time I knew exactly who the little girl was. She had been me. I had had an encounter with my inner child.

The term 'inner child' is a clichéd one but like a number of clichés it resonates with the truth. Carl Jung called it the 'Divine Child'. Emmet Fox called it the 'Wonder Child'. Charles Whitfield called it the 'Child Within'. Some psychotherapists call it the 'True Self'. But what is the inner child? The inner child is the child you once were who desired to be nurtured, cared for and loved. This child still resides within you as an adult. It is the part of you that is sensitive, creative, emotional, spontaneous, playful, intuitive, passionate, but it is also the part of you most in need of approval, comfort, guidance, love and reassurance. Many of us lose touch with our inner child as we leave childhood behind, but it remains with us all of our lives.

We are all children at heart, innocently searching for meaning in life, and it is through our inner child during times of crisis and challenge that our guardian angels often choose to reveal themselves to us. According to the Swedish mystic Emanuel Swedenborg there is no need to look outside ourselves to encounter angels because angels are within us, waiting to be discovered. My dream had shown me that it was through my inner child that my guardian angel was reaching out to me and telling me that I needed to look within myself for inspiration and guidance.

This was a lightbulb moment!

Why did I think so little of myself? That beautiful angel child in my dream made me see I was worth far more. The penny finally dropped. Maybe I was afraid of being left alone. Maybe I needed to be 'liked'. Maybe my relationships with other people had been damaged because I came from a broken home. Maybe my self-esteem was so low that I felt I didn't deserve better. I don't know why I had behaved in this way for so long, but it was time to stop blaming the past. It was time to start taking better care of myself. It was time to start expecting better treatment from others.

The feeling of relief was incredible, truly out of this world. In that instant, all the tension left my body and my face. It was as if I had been frowning all my life. I just relaxed in the comfort of my new understanding that my guardian angel lived inside and around me and I wasn't alone; a comfort that would always be there when the comfort of a partner or approval from others would not.

Needless to say, I didn't manage to hit my deadline that morning, but disaster didn't strike. My editor was disappointed but schedules were rearranged and I was given a two-week extension. And even if she had said I'd lost the job, it wouldn't have been the end of the world. You have no idea how powerful I felt after, perhaps for the first time in my life, not doing what was expected of me by others.

Trying to please others had defined my existence for so long that knowing I didn't need the approval of others did take time to fully sink in. In the months and years ahead, there were moments when I slipped back into my old ways, but I still look back on that night as an early breakthrough – the real turning point. Whenever old tensions and self-deprecating thoughts returned, I would force myself to head outside for a brisk walk. I would remind myself that my guardian angel loved me and I was worthy of that love. I didn't need the approval or acceptance of others. I wasn't being selfish if I had to say 'no' on occasion to the demands of others. I was lovingly reminding them that my life had value.

I can't say how long, or when exactly, I left my fears completely behind. I can only say that I did. Increasingly, I began to notice that the criticism or moodiness – or even the rejection – of others, affected me less and less. It wasn't that I didn't care about other people or what they thought; it was that I began to believe in myself, and to understand that if people ignored or rejected me it wasn't necessarily because they didn't like or want me, or because of something I had said or done, but was perhaps because of other things going on in their life. And if they didn't like or want me, well it's impossible to be all things to all people or to be liked by everyone without losing my personality in the process.

Was this progress down to my meeting with that mysterious lady on the Tube, my dream, my belief in the presence of my guardian angel, or simply because I was growing up and learning from the school of hard knocks? It was probably a combination of all these, along with a developing understanding that there was a spark of the divine within me and that my needs and my opinions were just as valuable as the needs and opinions of others. I also began to understand that over-attaching to the needs, feelings and lives of other people meant I had no life of my own. Looking to other people for good feelings about myself was like travelling in the back seat of a car. There was no sense of my own direction or purpose, no clarity. I could not head in the direction of the messages the angels inside and around me were sending about the purpose and meaning of my life.

Two years after my break-up the phone rang one day and it was my ex-boyfriend. He told me how much he missed me. Here, at last, were the words I had so longed to hear but they came too late – I had moved on. A tiny part of me struggled to rush back in, but the wiser part resisted. I listened with concern and love to his dilemmas, and thanked him for making amends, but I also told him that there was no going back. We had both moved on. After putting the phone down the feeling of lightness, hope and possibility was intoxicating. I got the same feeling when I quietly and gently let demanding or needy friends know that there were times when my own needs had to come first. Sure, I lost a few friends in the process, but the ones who really cared for me remained constant.

I remember one instance with a friend I had met at university. We had kept in touch on and off over the years, but it had always been on her terms. On more than one occasion, she had phoned me up to fix up a lunch meeting and then five or so minutes before, or worse still when I was actually sitting waiting in the restaurant, she cancelled on herself. She never apologized, just as she never apologized for always putting conversations on her mobile ahead of conversations with me. Silently and quietly, I had always put up with these 'putdowns', but with renewed faith in myself and my angels, I eventually found the courage to stop returning her calls and let her slip out of my life.

Yes, it took a while and I freely admit it was sometimes one step forward and two steps back, but with the help of my angels, I did gradually begin to understand that caring for my own needs was just as important as caring for the needs of others. At times it was even more important because if I could not love and cherish myself, how could I ever really love and cherish others?

This isn't to say I became selfish and ego-centred; that's a path no guardian angel would want anyone to walk. It's just that I learned a vitally important spiritual truth: there's a big difference between offering loving help and attention to someone in need, and totally ignoring your own needs in the process. There's also a huge difference between selflessly going out of your way to help others because your heart is filled with love and compassion for your fellow beings, and helping them because you want their approval or gratitude.

Another vitally important lesson I learned was that being a 'good' or 'spiritual' person isn't about being a doormat and always putting the needs of others above our own. Of course, our angels want us to reach out to other people and help lighten their loads if we can, but they also want us to honour and treat with reverence the angel, the spark of divinity, that lives within each one of us, and this means treating ourselves with love and kindness and, above all, respect.

Learning to love ourselves, not in an egotistical or selfish way, but in a spiritual way, is one of the hardest, but also one of the most essential, spiritual lessons to learn. Sadly, like me, many of us simply don't know how or where to begin. Everyone's path is different, but in my opinion one of the best ways to start is by reacquainting yourself with the child within you – the child who is in desperate need of love, nurturing and protection. However old you are, that child is still there, still in need of guidance and comfort; just waiting for you to take on the role of parent so you can grow in strength and courage and connect with the inner angel that can comfort, inspire and guide you.

I can now see that breaking my heart was an experience I needed to go through. It forced me to acknowledge and take care of the hurt and vulnerable child within me, the spark of hope and divinity within me I didn't think existed any more. Even though it hurt at the time and tore my heart out, I wouldn't change anything, as I have been able to accept the gift of that experience. At the time I thought it was the end of the world for me, but it wasn't. It was the beginning of a new dawn. Hindsight really is a great teacher in such situations.

Hindsight is a great teacher

Glancing back now at my life – I've just turned forty-five as I write this – I can see that there have been many times when I felt I was at an ending, that all hope was lost and that I would never be happy again. But each time there was a moment or an event or something miraculous that turned things around and brought me closer to the angels within and around me. More often than not I did not know my angels were at work, but now, with the benefit of age and hindsight, I can clearly see their footprints in my life. I may not have been ready to hear or see them, but my angels were with me all along, guiding, helping and inspiring me with dreams, coincidences, chance meetings and whispers of profound intuition.

One of the most wonderful things about getting older, and one of the reasons why I would never want to turn back the clock on my life, is looking back and seeing how all the pieces of the puzzle have fitted together. So often what you may have labelled as a great misfortune, trauma and crisis at the time was also an opportunity for you to make profound changes in your life, learn about yourself and discover a courage, hope and self-belief your never realized you had. And every time you connected with that courage, hope and power, what you were actually doing was rediscovering the angel within you. And when you begin to acquaint yourself with that angel the real magic begins, and you begin to see angels all around you, in everyone and everything.

While I was gathering together stories for this book, I wondered over and over again how many people there must be out there who, like me, have found themselves wondering if there is any meaning or purpose to their lives or if they have a guardian angel at all. I want to ask all those people to dig deep into their memories and their hearts. Remember, your angels are unlikely to have appeared in the traditional manner. Perhaps you had a hunch or an insight that changed your mind and your life? Perhaps a coincidence changed everything for the better? Perhaps the kind words, or actions, of a stranger or a loved one helped you through a rough patch? Perhaps the loving companionship of a pet brought you joy and love when you needed it the most?

If you're convinced that none of the above applies to you, nothing astonishing has happened to you, and you have never seen or felt an angel, then perhaps reading this book will be the turning point. Perhaps it will help you become more aware of the subtle ways in which angels weave their wonder and magic in your life. Perhaps it will help you see that you are indeed entertaining angels unaware, that there is an eternal divine spark within.

I was born into a family of psychics and spiritualists – my mother heard and spoke to angels all her life – so, of all people, you would have thought that I'd have had a close connection with the world of spirit from an early age. But this wasn't the case at all. In my childhood and early adult life I tried so very hard to see angels, but nothing came through. It's only really been in the last ten or so years that I've become fully aware of the way that angels work in my life. For so long I felt like a failure, because I did not have the 'gift', and this was especially the case when I could not even connect with my mum in spirit when she died. I'd been closer to her than anyone, so if I couldn't connect with her, I really was a lost cause. But, again with the benefit of hindsight, I can now see that I wasn't meant to see anything until I was older.

You see, if it had always been easy for me to see angels – if I had levitated in my cot or seen dead people in the high street – I might never have been able to understand or relate to all the people who have written to me over the years telling me they think there is something wrong with them because they can't see spirits. I might never have been able to give these people hope and guidance. I might never have been able to use my own experience and frustrations as a springboard for my books. I might never have been able to say with absolute conviction that anyone, even ordinary people like you and me, can see angels. I might never have been able to convey the important message of this book – that spiritual development and psychic awareness and the life transformation that results can only ever truly begin from *within*.

The truth is, until recently I wasn't ready to see my angels because I couldn't see them inside myself first. I needed to let go of my inner conflicts, because fear and low self-esteem are natural predators of the angels. I needed to learn to stop trying to be everything to everyone. I needed to trust and respect myself and to learn from my mistakes, instead of beating myself up about them. I needed to learn that even though I am not perfect, there is goodness and the potential for greatness in me.

Most important of all, I needed to believe in miracles and to accept that sometimes, for reasons I may never understand while I am on earth, unfair and cruel things happen to innocent and good people. I can do all I can to help and ease the suffering of · others, but when this isn't enough I need to simply trust that the powers of love and goodness will always be stronger than those of darkness. I need to trust that sometimes it is only in death that the dawn follows the darkness. In short, I need to trust and let my angels lead me through this life and the next.

Ever since I've become aware of angels within and around me, I've noticed profound changes in my life. Everything has just started to add up and make sense. This isn't, of course, to say that I don't have any problems or setbacks any more. I have my fair share of hang-ups, setbacks and self-doubts, just like everyone else. Some days I wake up and feel like banging my head and my keyboard in frustration, but what has changed is that I have learned to stop being frightened by change. I am willing to learn and grow from it, not feel threatened by it. I'm willing to see the positive in everyone and everything, including myself, because I know my angels only see what is good and loving in me.

There have been many other moments in my life when angels have changed my world. As mentioned previously, some of these moments have only been recognized with the gift of hindsight, while the miraculous nature of others was blindingly obvious at the time. I do hope sharing some of my experiences here will have helped you better understand me and my passion for writing about angels.

I'd dearly love to share more of my stories with you here, but not only does space prevent this, the heart of this book also prevents it because the heart of this book – and the remaining chapters – belong not to me but to the remarkable people who have got in touch with me over the years to contribute their unusual, unexpected and dramatic stories. I hope you will be as inspired and as comforted as I always am by their contributions. The first few chapters will continue the theme of this chapter – divine flashes of insight or inspiration that in seconds quite literally turn a person's life around, before moving on to other life-changing glimpses of heaven on earth. The remaining chapters will focus on stories of transformation inspired by dreams, angel signs and encounters with departed loved ones in spirit.

Angel stories are reminders that goodness and love remain real and powerful forces in our everyday lives. They are also proof that even though we can't always see it, our world is connected with the world of spirit and all we need to do to make contact with that magical and wonderful world is believe in it and allow ourselves to become aware of its divine presence in our hearts and in our lives. So, as you move on with this book, be prepared to be both astonished and reminded by the words that fly off the pages. Astonished by the sheer unexpectedness of the stories and the infinite number of ways angels can reach down into our mortal lives and affect changes. And reminded of something you once knew, but may have forgotten along the way, that your life is a magical journey that doesn't end with death.

Calling all angels

Finally, just before you turn the page, if you have had any angel experiences, I'd like to encourage you to share them with me (details about how you can do so can be found on page 234 of this book) or with other people. The more people share stories of angels with each other the easier it is for the angels to fly close to earth and bring with them their awesome love and goodness. Remember, angels often appear in the most unlikely disguises or in ways that we recognize only with the benefit of hindsight. The lady who gave me such sage advice on the Tube train that day after I had broken up with my boyfriend, and the insightful dream I had a while later – these were not full-blown angel sightings complete with wings and halo, but I have no doubt that they were divinely inspired. As I always say in my books, if you aren't sure if you have heard, seen or felt an angel, trust your heart; it will always know the answer, because love is the only language the angels speak. Don't waste time and energy, as I did, by letting low self-esteem and disbelief prevent you from seeing the magic within and around you. Instead, trust the angels within and all around you and see how that trust can change your life.

Never lose sight of the reality that your angels are always with you in one way or another, and the more you believe and the more you notice and remember them, the more they will reveal themselves to you. An inspirational moment, unexpected feelings of happiness, a sense of peace and serenity, the kindness of a stranger or a loved one, warm-hearted laughter or anything that brings you feelings of joy are all places where your angels can be found, but remember, there are so many other astonishing ways in which angels can transform your world. Just keep your mind, your eyes and your heart open, let go of notions and expectations of what angels should and should not be, and always expect the unexpected.

Trust me, the more you can suspend disbelief, and the more you are able to live your life with an attitude of gratitude, respect and love, the more everything and everyone in your life will be changed for the eternal good.

Seize your moment. This is your time for new beginnings.

CHAPTER 2

Thunderbolts and Lightning

Gratitude bestows reverence, allowing us to encounter everyday epiphanies, those transcendent moments of awe that change forever how we experience life and the world.

John Milton

Have you ever had a sudden or unexplainable change of heart and wondered, 'Where did that come from! That's the last thing I thought I would do or agree to?' That's the work of your angels guiding you in the direction you need to go. Have you ever felt completely wretched, feeling that a situation is hopeless and impossible to change and then suddenly out of nowhere the obvious solution appears? You are filled with hope and optimism. It's your angels at work again. And have you ever felt forgotten and alone and then a warm feeling unexpectedly engulfs and revitalizes you? That's the touch of an angel to let you know you are not alone.

Sometimes a life can be changed by one single inspiration, feeling, thought, or idea. From out of nowhere a sudden sense of understanding of the world, and your place in it, as though everything is as it should be, emerges. There is a feeling that everything in the world is in its rightful place. The religious terminology for such an experience is an epiphany. I'm reluctant to use this word so early on in the book because for many people it has such strong religious connotations, referring to the manifestation of a divine being. I'm reluctant because although angels can fit perfectly with any belief system, they are truly non-denominational. I prefer, therefore, for now to call these experiences 'realizations', 'inspirations' or those divine 'thunderbolts and lightning' moments when everything in the world makes sense and fits together.

All the stories collected together for you in this chapter show how, more often than not, such life-changing realizations are angel-inspired. In some cases it was later in their lives that the angelic origin of such moments was recognized by the people who experienced them, but for others this was not the case. They knew exactly what they were experiencing at the time it occurred.

As well as being perfect examples of divine guidance, the stories also show how in many cases it seems as if a whole life has been leading or feeding into one brief moment, which emerges as the catalyst for change. I can't help but think that if we could all regard each moment of our lives as a potential opportunity for change and growth, then it would become so much easier to keep our minds open to the possibilities that may cross our path. In other words, if we could live each moment as if it was potentially the moment that transformed our lives for ever, then our lives would have a richness and a spiritual depth that may have previously been lacking.

In recent years, there have been many occasions, usually when I've been buried in my work or the routines of my day-to-day life, when suddenly a profound feeling, thought or inspiration washes over me and I'm reminded and reassured once again that my guardian angel is forever by my side.

One occasion stands out in particular, and it happened fairly recently in the supermarket, of all places. I was putting items in my basket and feeling a little stressed because, as usual, the basket was getting very full and very heavy. I was also running late to pick up my kids from school, and my mobile phone was ringing. I put my basket down and tried to find my phone. I could hear it ringing, but it wasn't in my pockets or in my bag. Then I remembered it was in the bottom of my shopping basket. In my haste to answer the phone I knocked over the eggs and smashed them on the floor. Undeterred by this setback I grabbed my phone, only to find it was yet another home-insurance quote call I didn't want.

Annoyed, I picked up my basket and looked around to alert a sales assistant to the broken eggs on the floor. Then I realized that I had put my bag onto the broken eggs and there was egg yolk all down my coat and trousers. I could feel myself getting very angry and tense. I was going to be late. I had so much to do, this really wasn't fair.

Still angry and stressed, I managed to get to the checkout, but just before I did I nearly bumped into a kind-looking gentle-man. We both offered each other an opportunity to go through the checkout first, but he insisted I go, so I did. While I was packing my bags, I noticed that he was with two other people and they had obvious learning difficulties. They kept trying to hug him and were rearranging food items in his basket, but gently and quietly he kept everything and everyone in order. He was one of the most refined and calm people I have ever seen.

As I left the store I took one last look at the gentleman and he had a quiet smile on his face. In an instant I felt all my previous tension replaced by a wave of happiness. It wasn't just because he had put my own little 'stresses' in perspective; it was because his warmth and patience had triggered intense feelings of euphoria, possibility and hope in me. He had reminded me of the divine potential for compassion, love and greatness that is within us all, and how we are all capable of rising above the frustrations, traumas and challenges of daily life. How we are all capable of living in a way that our guardian angel would approve.

There have been many other moments like this in my life; moments when time stands still, confusion and stress recede and heightened feelings of happiness, profundity, insight, understanding, hope and inspiration take over. I know during these moments that my angels are closer to me than ever before. It's almost as if they are lifting me up, inspiring me to believe in the impossible.

These moments can strike at any time, often when we least expect them. This was certainly the case for Ruby, whose moving story follows on below.

Paint a rainbow

Charlotte was only four years old when she died. I think about her every second of every day. I miss her every time my heart beats but the grief and torment I felt has been replaced by a sense of comfort. Let me explain.

Charlotte was fantastic at drawing for one so young. She was forever scribbling and handing me pictures of stick men and women. In the months before she died she'd include rainbows in almost all of her pictures. She'd even draw snowmen with rainbows hovering over them. When I asked her why, she just laughed and said that you can have rainbows anywhere you want to.

I don't want to go into the details of her unexpected death as some things hurt so much and are best unsaid, but I do want to tell you about her funeral. I woke up on the day of her funeral numb with shock and aching with grief. My mum had to help me get dressed as I was shaking so much and could barely stand. I wanted my little girl back. I would have given my life to have my little girl back. I regretted all those times I had sent her back to bed when she couldn't sleep. Why hadn't I held her; savoured every precious second? I longed for some kind of sign from her that she was OK and that she was in a place where there was only love and joy. I prayed for a sign, but resigned myself to the fact that I wasn't going to get one. Real life didn't work that way.

It was raining hard as we drove towards the church but I barely noticed. Everything seemed bleak and grey now; the world had lost its colour without her in it and even if the sun had been out it would still have felt like rain to me. We stood there with our umbrellas as her little coffin was lowered into the grave. My legs felt weak and I sank to the ground sobbing. People gathered round to help me up but I didn't want to get up. I wanted to sink into the earth.

It was my mother who forced me to look up. She lifted my chin and told me to open my eyes and there was the most stunning rainbow I have ever seen. The colours were vivid, bright and intense and the more I looked at it the more the colours sparkled. The rainbow was so lovely I knew it was Charlotte speaking to me. I got up and looked over at the street that ran past the cemetery. People were stopping their cars and getting out of them to gaze at the rainbow. I've never seen a rainbow so intense and colourful since.

The world stood still for me that moment and colour came back into my life again. I hugged my two other children and told them that wherever we were in the world Charlotte would be with us, smiling down on us, reminding us that you can see rainbows anywhere.

For Ruby, a simple rainbow instantly transformed her grief. Of course, some people might interpret this story differently, but any person who has lost a child or a loved one will know differently. When the angels see our pain they can pour comfort into our grieving hearts by revealing themselves to us in ordinary but extraordinary ways. In this way without causing alarm or distress they can show us clearly and personally that we are not alone and those we have lost are here with us right now, in every moment of our lives, in every bit of creation.

Like Ruby, Jessica's story below shows that transcendent moments can not only adjust our view of this life, but can also adjust our views of the other side.

Seeing the light

I'm writing to tell you about something that happened to me six years ago. It's about my father. I'd just left school and was looking forward to my hairdressing training when my father suffered a series of strokes. Mum and Dad were separated and I was an only child so I put my career on hold to take care of him. I did it because I love my dad, but he was a very heavily built man and helping him move about took it out of me. As well as caring for him I had to do all the cleaning and errands and run the household. It was exhausting. A part of me also resented the fact that I had had to put my life on hold. A part of me wanted to be young and carefree.

One evening I was sitting next to Dad while he slept in his armchair. I was just about to doze off myself when I was jolted awake by this strong awareness that my late grandmother was with us. I'd never met my grandmother as she died giving birth to my dad. She wasn't present in any visual or auditory sense but in my mind and my heart I knew she was there. She was speaking to me, telling me that she would be there to help me and also to help my father cross over.

Through it all my father remained asleep. I felt so moved and reassured that I went outside into the garden. Just as I did the sun came out and warmed my face. It was a deeply moving experience. There were tears in my eyes. I had quite literally seen the light. I knew that I would be able to cope and that I wasn't alone.

In the weeks that followed the strong feeling that my grandmother was present stayed with me. I didn't feel tired or resentful or tied down any more. I can't explain it but everything seemed easier. It really did feel as if I was being helped. My dad's doctor was surprised by how upbeat I was considering the amount of work I had to do.

I felt hesitant about telling my dad about my experience. I wasn't sure how he would take it, but when I did he wasn't surprised in any way. He told me that he had been thinking a lot about the mum he never knew. He also felt her closeness. Six months later my dad died. I was heartbroken but also comforted by the thought that he was reunited with his mother in spirit.

Before that experience I had never really believed in life after death but from that point on everything changed. I sensed the presence of my grandmother for only a few brief moments, but those few moments were enough to change my mind and my life for ever. I have absolutely no doubt now that there are angels watching over me, however tough my life gets.

Monica's experience also gave her a new understanding of this life, and the next:

Beating myself up

My partner – the love of my life – died two years ago. I miss him beyond imagination. I didn't think I could carry on. We'd been married only a year and I had a baby on the way when he died. The most horrible thing of all was that I blamed myself. You see, he'd wanted to use the car that day to go on a training exercise, but I had to go visit my mum and I needed it too. He phoned his friend who said he would pick him up on his motorbike and I got to use the car. The motorbike crashed and I never got to say goodbye.

Jake was serving in the army, so I guess you get used to living with the possibility of loss, but not loss when he's at home, on his leave. When I got the news I was completely numb. Then about a week later, after the funeral, the tears started and didn't stop. I felt wretched and hopeless. I thought about dying. I hated the fact that I was pregnant. I didn't think I had any love left to give my child. Worst of all I felt such guilt. If only I had let him use the car that day. If only.

After a few weeks of beating myself up, my mum forced me to move back in with her. I wasn't eating properly and I certainly wasn't sleeping. Then one night everything changed. I was sitting on my bed looking through my favourite photos of Jake when I had what I can only describe as a vision. It wasn't a dream because I know I was awake. As soon as the vision was over I knew what it meant. I knew Jake hadn't left me and I would be OK. The vision was short and so real. It didn't happen in my mind's eye. I saw it playing out in front of me, like it was on a projector screen. In my vision I saw myself beating a child. I looked angry and the child was in clear distress. All of a sudden this beautiful lady – she didn't have wings but I knew she was an angel – appeared and put her arms around both me and the child. The beating and crying stopped.

In a flash the vision was gone and so was the weight of pain, guilt and anger I had felt. My angel had found me and it wanted me to forgive myself, to stop beating myself up. After that incredible moment I got my life back on track again. I discovered a courage and positivity in myself I didn't know I had. I still miss Jake every breath I take but I also know that he hasn't died. He is with the angels watching over me and he is living on inside little Jake, his son.

31

Ann's experience, below, is closer to what many people might describe as an epiphany in the religious sense, in that her experience involved a renewal of her faith.

An angel healed me

After reading *An Angel Healed Me* I feel I must write to you to tell you about my wonderful experience. I remarried for the second time to a man I thought loved me. To keep my story brief, I soon discovered that he married me for a better life in England. He treated me with contempt. After nearly four years I filed for divorce. Feeling absolutely wretched, exhausted and alone, I prayed to my angels for guidance for the future, I so feared for myself and for my baby daughter.

One day I was in my solicitor's office having to relive the past four years, which was quite traumatic. While I was talking I noticed some drawings of angels on the office wall. I asked and found out they had been drawn by my solicitor's five-year-old daughter. This led us into a conversation about angels. At that moment another solicitor called Mary came into the office. She also had a firm belief in angels and, seeing how tense I was discussing my divorce, she put a comforting hand on my shoulder.

As soon as her hand was on my shoulder all the tension left my body and I had the most incredible experience. I saw beautiful swirling colours before my eyes and lots of my favourite colour, purple. Suddenly, the colours stopped and there in front of me hovered a brilliant white robed man, Christ-like. Beside him sat a very fat jolly man wearing a beautiful robe. The jolly man was laughing but the

Christ-like man looked so serious. I thought at first I had upset him but then he turned his palms towards me and gave me a hint of a smile. I sensed love coming from his hands, face and robe. I don't know long my vision lasted but suddenly I was back in the 'real world'.

I started to cry. My worried solicitor asked why and I told her of the great happiness, joy and love coming from the angels, something I had never experienced with such power before. I can honestly say I felt honoured and privileged and from that day on I lost my fear for the future and for my daughter. I also felt that I should share this wonderful experience with you as nothing would make me happier than to know that it can give comfort and inspiration to others.

Angels, remember, are simply loving 'beings of light'. They are truly non-denominational and can fit into any belief system. They can also reach out to those of us who believe in something, but aren't sure what and even to those who before their moment of realization had no belief at all. That's why I'm going to follow on here with Angie's story. It differs from Ann's in that there isn't any religious imagery, but it is similar in that it also involved 'blinding light' and a rediscovery or renewal of spiritual belief and faith.

An unforgettable night

I would like to tell you about an experience I had while reading your book *An Angel Healed Me*. I will say I had never really considered the thought of angels but your book I found captivating and very hard to put down; it was also heart-warming.

I was reading your book in bed one night. I was about halfway through at the time. I settled down to sleep and then during the night – I had no idea of time but it was pitch-black – I was lying on my back and felt my right arm gently lift into the air. I turned my head and the chest of drawers was lit up by a bright light from under the bed. I didn't feel scared or uncomfortable or even have the urge to get up and investigate. I just went into a peaceful sleep.

I believe an angel visited me as before this experience I had been feeling fretful and anxious about my life. Since that unforgettable night my life seems calmer. Or should I say my life hasn't changed but I have; I'm calmer now. Issues I had don't seem to bother me now. I'm at peace. I'm looking forward to more encounters and I find myself talking to my angels from time to time.

Before her experience, Jenny, who tells her story below, had never regarded herself as spiritual but then, like all the people in this chapter, one single profound moment made her see her life and everything and everyone she encountered in a new way.

Breakthrough

My parents were atheists and I grew up believing I was one too. I was taught the value of kindness, compassion, and honesty. It all made perfect sense to me, and I just couldn't relate to people who went to church or had a belief system. For me, it was the here and now that mattered; everything else was idle speculation.

Everything changed for me one day when I was teaching my Year 5 class. I'm a primary-school teacher and I was talking to them about a book I wanted them to read together over the term. It's called *Skellig* by David Almond and a lot of people think it may be about an angel. Now, my Year 5 class was a notoriously difficult class to teach. I'd been struggling to connect with them ever since I took over from the previous teacher a few weeks ago. She'd resigned because of stress and that kind of said it all. They weren't bad kids, just unruly and lacking in discipline. At times I found my role was more about classroom management than teaching. I love teaching and not making any progress was frustrating me. I was looking for a breakthrough. I had no idea at the time that this was the day it was going to happen, not just for them but for me.

I started talking to them about the book and the angel theme in it. I half expected most of them to laugh or switch off as they normally do, but something felt very different. I teach in a multicultural, multi-religion school and a large percentage of the kids have learning difficulties or come from broken homes, but I'm not joking — as soon as I started talking about angels, they started listening. I could not believe it. Not one of the kids was interrupting me or messing about. It was bliss. I could teach, at last.

After talking a while and enjoying their concentration, I asked them what they thought about angels and whether or not they believed in them. Without exception virtually every hand in the class shot up, even the hands of those who rarely bothered to engage with me. Seizing the opportunity, I asked them all to draw me a picture of an angel and then write down what they thought angels were. They settled down immediately to the task and each and every one of them handed me a picture and a few lines of writing before the bell for break rang.

As the children walked – instead of their usual running and pushing – out of the classroom I had a moment of profound and life-changing realization. I realized that although there was nothing wrong with my humanistic approach to life, there was a huge gap in my understanding of why I believed humans should be good to one another, and how we should be good in the world. With absolute clarity the reaction of my pupils had shown me that there is within each of us something that is spiritual and separate from what is human. And one of the reasons why I hadn't been connecting with my pupils was that I had focused only on their human needs and ignored their spiritual ones. By reaching out to their spiritual needs that lesson I had finally found a way to unite them as a class and to connect them with me. I felt an unfamiliar warmth and a lightness about me as I sat there watching the children running about in the playground.

From that day on I began to open myself up to the spiritual side of humanity. I stopped looking at the differences between myself and others and instead reached out to our shared need for a connection to the divine within and around us. Since I took that leap of faith, everything in my life has become easier. My Year 5 class certainly aren't perfect, but we've bonded and I do feel that I'm getting through to them, which as any teacher will tell you is pretty much a miracle these days. I have the angels to thank for that.

Richard also came to a new understanding following a moment of inspiration. Indeed, his experience overturned every expectation he had ever had of how he should live his life.

Another coffee?

Five years ago I lived life in the fast lane. I worked in the City. I can't go into the details because that wouldn't be fair to the people I used to work with, but for the purposes of your book I think all you need to know is that it was a highly competitive environment, with big rewards and payouts. There was also quite a lot of backstabbing, but everybody just accepted this as part of the culture we worked in.

I can remember the day my life changed exactly. It was the seventeenth of June and it was very hot and sunny. I decided to step outside the office for a coffee break – I used to be addicted to the stuff – and also to take some time out. I'd been working at my desk since seven a.m. and it was almost eleven a.m. and I hadn't taken a break. In fact I hadn't taken a break for the last two years. My life revolved around work. Don't get me wrong. I wasn't complaining. There were plenty of rewards and loads of perks – a company car, stunning accommodation, a six-figure salary and so on. In my mind, I was thinking another ten years of this and I'd be able to retire early.

Anyway, I headed down to a nearby cafe in the street, ordered an iced coffee and went to sit outside. I sat down and then realized I had forgotten to bring the folder with me that I was going to look through as I had my coffee. I felt angry because it was urgent and also because I hated sitting in cafes with nothing to read or look at. It made me look a bit lonely and sad.

There was nothing I could do, so I just sat there and drank my coffee. With nothing to keep my mind and eyes occupied, I looked around me at all the people on the other tables. Some were deep in conversation, others were reading or working, everyone looked very

37

busy. I was the only one just sitting there with nothing to do. For a few moments I fidgeted but then all of a sudden this feeling of stillness and calm came over me. I watched some birds hopping around under the tables. I got fascinated watching them.

While I was sitting there I had this feeling that all my worries were leaving me. For the first time in years I felt calm and completely happy. The waitress passed by and asked me if I wanted another coffee. I said yes and sat there for another hour, not really thinking about anything, just enjoying watching and listening to what was going on around me.

Instead of leaving to go back to work, I stayed at the cafe and had another coffee and then lunch. And then I had dessert. My phone kept buzzing with texts and calls, but I switched it off. I didn't make a conscious decision. I just knew deep down that I wasn't going back to my job. I didn't want to go back. The more I thought about my lifestyle, the more I realized how empty and self-serving it was and that I wouldn't know happiness until I changed my life.

When it came to settling my bill, I couldn't believe my eyes when I noticed that my server's name was Angel. How incredible is that?

After that day, I resigned and took a few months to get my head together. I did a lot of thinking and soul searching and am now working for a charity. I'm throwing my energies into helping others, not just myself, but I also give myself plenty of time to enjoy the sunshine and smell the flowers. I still head down to that cafe from time to time to sit outside on the street and watch the world go by. My girlfriend, Lucy, believes in angels and it was she who encouraged me to send my story to you. I hope you enjoy reading it as much as I have enjoyed writing it down for you.

For Richard, a moment of profound realization brought him a new understanding of what it means to be happy. His story shows that angels can take us on journeys we didn't know we needed to go on and transform our lives in the most unexpected of ways. In translation, the word 'angel' actually means 'messenger', and because the life-changing messages angels bring are always those of wisdom, guidance and inspiration they are also teachers. Perhaps, like Richard, we should all take a step back from our lives now and again to reconsider how we understand happiness, and whether or not the things in our lives which we define as good things are really the true source of happiness.

As with Richard, a moment of profound realization also brought George, whose story is below, a new understanding of what it means to be happy. As you'll see it took a while for George to fully understand the messages sent to him from the other side. There was a gradual build-up of angel-inspired signs and encounters all leading up to one dramatic moment.

Heaven scent

I used to live the perfect life. I think a lot of people must have thought of me in terms of success. I had my own business, which was doing very well indeed. I had a gorgeous and roomy house in a quiet suburb and a holiday home in Spain. Then there was my beautiful wife and three grown-up children; all three of my kids were a credit and a joy to me. One was at medical school and the other two were forging successful careers in the City. I had lots of good friends and was blessed with good health. I guess you could say my cup was overflowing; but now looking back I can see that I wasn't really as happy as I convinced myself I was.

The house seemed very quiet when the last of my children left. Instead of coming to terms with this new phase in my life, taking time out to reflect and deal with my feelings of loss and fear of getting old, I worked harder than ever before. It was like I needed to keep busy to avoid the silence at home and to prove to myself and everyone else that I was still up-and-coming and not ready for life in the slow lane. I invested in several properties at home and abroad and expanded my business. I treated myself to my dream car – a ludicrously expensive Porsche I didn't really need – got my hair dyed back to its original chestnut brown and even had a few nips and tucks on my growing belly.

Then one Sunday afternoon I was invited, along with my wife, to a party held by Alan, my oldest friend. In the early years of setting up my business Alan had been a real support. He had lent me money when the banks turned me down. I had paid him back many times over since, but for his generosity when I needed it the most I was forever in his debt.

When I got to the party it was a polite and well-dressed occasion, but there was one person who just looked so out of place. Sitting hunched and dishevelled in cheap-looking clothes in a corner by himself was a middle-aged man with a startled look on his face. I noticed shaving cuts all over his chin. I knew most of Alan's friends very well, as we were a close-knit set, but I had no idea who this man was. The man seemed to sense my interest in and confusion about him and before I could tear my eyes away he got up out of his seat and started to wobble — it wasn't a walk — towards me. When he got closer he held out his hand and introduced himself as Thomas. I had no choice but to offer my hand even though it was the last thing I felt like doing, and told him my name was George. Once he had got hold of my hand Thomas didn't seem to want to let go. He smiled broadly at me with a yellow set of teeth.

I was convinced he was drunk or a bit simple, but when he held my hand the smell that hit me wasn't alcohol but lavender soap. I remember thinking how odd it was for someone to look that untidy and unkempt to smell so fresh. I looked around anxiously, hoping that Alan would come and rescue me, but he was deep in conversation with someone else. So I gritted my teeth and talked politely about the weather, before excusing myself to use the restroom.

I did my best to avoid any eye contact with Thomas for the rest of the afternoon. I didn't want to be trapped again. I spent my time chatting to my friends and tucking into the buffet. When it was time to leave Alan took me aside and asked me if I could do something for him. He told me that for the past few months he had joined a volunteer group and he was giving Thomas a ride every day from his doctor back to his care home. Problem was he was soon going away on holiday and he needed someone to taxi Thomas for ten days while he was away.

I glanced at Thomas nodding off in the same corner of the room he had been when I first saw him and politely but firmly told Alan that I'd love to help out but right now wasn't a good time for me. I had the new properties to manage and so much going on at work. There just weren't enough hours in the day. Alan looked disappointed so I tried to make a joke of it and said something along the lines of: 'Have pity, mate. I've just bought a brand-new Porsche. It's my pride and joy. No offence, but this guy would cramp my style.'

Alan was such a laid-back guy and had so many friends I was sure he would just shrug his shoulders and ask someone else, but what he did next really surprised me. He grabbed my arm, looked me straight in the eye and told me that it wasn't much of my time that Thomas needed and besides I owed him. To say I was shocked is an understatement. In all our years of friendship Alan had never used emotional blackmail before. I didn't like it and told him in no uncertain terms that I didn't want anything to do with Thomas. You could have cut the atmosphere with a knife as Alan and I said our goodbyes with pursed lips and a stilted handshake.

The following afternoon I took my beloved Porsche out for a spin. It was a beautiful day and I felt very contented and smug, until I became aware of this overpowering smell of lavender. At first I thought it came from outside so I stopped the car and got out, but outside the air smelled fine. The lavender scent was definitely coming from inside the car. I drove home and asked my wife to see what she thought, but she said she couldn't smell anything and didn't know what I was talking about. For the next few days every time I got inside my Porsche I was hit by the strong smell of lavender. I had no idea what was causing it. On one occasion I thought the smell had gone but within five or ten minutes of driving I felt like I was in a perfumery.

The weekend after Alan's party I got a phone call from Alan himself. He seemed to have forgotten our tense conversation and begged me just this one time to collect Thomas from the doctor, because his wife was under the weather and needed him to stay at home with her. He said I really was his last resort and he had called around asking other people first but nobody could do it. He said I was his last hope. I was so happy to hear from him that I surprised myself by saying yes. I drove to the doctor's feeling good that I had made amends but a little ticked off that Alan had finally got his way.

When I arrived at the surgery I saw Thomas waiting outside. He mumbled some words of thanks as he got into the car and shuffled around a bit until he got comfortable. I had to remind him to put on his seatbelt and it brought back memories of asking my children to do the same. Throughout the journey I glanced anxiously at him and once again this brought back memories of my children. He took great delight in putting the window up and down and watched the passing scenery with curiosity and excitement. When I arrived at the care home, he said his thanks again. I watched him shuffle into the care centre and then drove slowly home. I was so taken up with thoughts of Thomas and how his life must be in that care home that it was only when I got home that I realized that the lavender smell was stronger than ever in my car – I must have got used to it.

The experience hadn't been nearly as inconvenient or as unsavoury as I had thought it might be so when Alan called that evening to ask how things went, I found myself offering to be Thomas's taxi for the next ten days while Alan went on holiday.

Something incredible and unexplainable happened to me during those ten days. Gradually, Thomas and I began to connect. I called him by his name and he called me by mine. He didn't say much but when he did speak his words were well chosen and always thought-provoking. On the final day I asked him if he would like to go for a drink. You see, I was actually starting to enjoy the company of this guy. In the pub I could see other people reacting to him in much the same way I must have done at Alan's party, but that didn't matter to me any more. He was my friend.

I couldn't believe how sad I felt when I dropped Thomas off for the last time and told him that Alan would be back the next day. I also can't believe how what he said next went straight to my heart. 'Thanks, mate,' he replied. 'People never cease to surprise me. I had you down as a guy who only thought about himself. I was wrong. That will teach me to judge others by the way they look.'

I just could not believe what I heard Thomas say. As he walked into the care home I sat down in my car and had the biggest reality check of my life. I was the one who thought I was judging, but the reality was it was always the other way round. I was the one who had got it all wrong. How could I have been so blind? In that moment, I can honestly say my understanding of myself and my life and the way I was living it changed for ever.

When Alan got back from his holiday I asked him to tell me a bit about Thomas and how he had ended up in a care home. Alan told me that Thomas had once been a highly respected surgeon but his career and his marriage came to an end when he was hit by a cyclist five years ago. The accident had left him with head, leg and back injuries from which he would never recover. He had no living relatives or family to take care of him. He required daily medical monitoring and daily medication. He had seizures quite regularly, wobbled when he walked and definitely couldn't drive.

Alan went on to tell me that he had witnessed one of the relentless seizures Thomas suffered from. During the seizure Thomas had lost control of his bodily functions and vomited on himself before losing consciousness. Paramedics had to be called to clean him up and get him back on his feet. Thomas felt deeply embarrassed by these incidents, and concerned that other people might be bothered by unpleasant smells, so he over-compensated by zealously washing and using bottles and bottles of lavender fabric conditioner on his clothes.

The next day and the days after driving in my Porsche just didn't seem so fantastic or exciting any more. I had this amazing car, and a life many would envy, but there was emptiness inside me. I really missed helping Thomas and making a difference to his day. Helping him had ignited feelings within me that I had thought were long dead. I don't know how but he made me feel young again.

So, I ended up calling Alan and asking to share the rides with Thomas. Alan was delighted at my change of heart and readily agreed. For the next year and a half Thomas became a part of my daily routine and my life.

Thomas died some ten years ago, but to this day his lavender scent is indelibly inscribed in my senses. I really met him against my will. If it were my choice I never would have allowed this helpless, scary and unkempt-looking man into my precious car and into my comfortable, busy life. But Thomas taught me that angels can appear in many different forms and in circumstances you cannot ever expect or anticipate. He taught me that at any age there are ways to feel young, purposeful and fulfilled again.

I have no idea to this day why my car smelled so strongly of lavender before he got into it. All I know is that the scent of lavender changed the life of a man suffering from a debilitating case of self-centredness and a critical case of hardness of heart by teaching him to open his heart and his mind. That man was me.

George and Richard's profound stories remind me of an email sent to me by Greg a couple of years ago which is also about a person changing their mind and their whole approach to life. It's a story I often find myself revisiting, I hope you will too.

Don't we all?

I was parked in front of the shopping centre wiping off my car. I had just come from the car wash and was waiting for my wife to get out of work. Coming my way from across the car park was what society would consider a bum. From the looks of him, he had no car, no home, no clean clothes, and no money. There are times when you feel generous but there are other times that you just don't want to be bothered. This was one of those 'don't want to be bothered' times.

'I hope he doesn't ask me for any money,' I thought. He didn't. He came and sat on the kerb in front of the bus stop but he didn't look like he could have enough money to even ride the bus. After a few minutes he spoke.

'That's a very pretty car,' he said.

He was ragged but he had an air of dignity about him. I said, 'Thanks,' and continued wiping off my car. He sat there quietly as I worked. The expected plea for money never came. As the silence between us widened something inside said, 'Ask him if he needs any help.' I was sure that he would say yes but I held true to the inner voice.

'Do you need any help?' I asked.

He answered in three simple but profound words that I shall never forget. We often look for wisdom in great men and women.

We expect it from those of higher learning and accomplishments. I expected nothing but an outstretched, grimy hand. He spoke three words that shook me.

'Don't we all?' he said.

I was feeling high and mighty, successful and important, above a bum in the street, until those three words hit me like a twelve-gauge shotgun. Don't we all? Yes, I needed help. Maybe not for bus fare or a place to sleep, but I needed help. I reached in my wallet and gave him not only enough for bus fare, but enough to get a warm meal and shelter for the day. Those three little words still ring true. No matter how much you have, no matter how much you have accomplished, you need help too. No matter how little you have, no matter how loaded you are with problems, even without money or a place to sleep, you can give help, even if it's just a smile or a compliment.

Everyone, however much they appear to have it all, may be waiting for others to help give them what they don't have. It could be a different perspective on life, a glimpse of something beautiful, a respite from daily chaos that only you through a torn world can see. Maybe the man was just a homeless stranger wandering the streets. Maybe he was more than that. Maybe he was sent by a power that is great and wise, to minister to a soul too comfortable in himself. Maybe God looked down, called an angel, dressed him like a bum, then said, 'Go minister to that man cleaning the car, that man needs help.'

Don't we all?

I wrote back immediately to thank Greg for sending me this profound story for inclusion in my angel books. He never replied, so I don't know if it really happened to him, as it did for the other people in this book, or if it is more of an allegory, but in many ways it does not really matter because if the story inspires you to open your mind and see yourself and others in a different light, then in my mind it is truly angelic.

Now I'd like to draw your attention to something astonishing I read in the press earlier this year. I'm including it here because it shows once again how angels can reveal themselves through surprising moments of life-changing divine insight.

The biggest shock of my life

In February 2010 Austrian millionaire Karl Rabeder decided to give away his £3 million fortune after realizing his riches were making him unhappy. According to media reports Mr Rabeder, 47, a business-man from Telfs, put his luxury 3,455 sq ft villa with lake, sauna and spectacular Alpine views, valued at £1.4 million, up for sale. Also for sale was his stone farmhouse in Provence with its 17 hectares over-looking the arrière-pays, on the market for a cool £613,000. Already sold was his collection of six gliders (£350,000), and a luxury Audi A8 (£44,000) and the interior furnishings and accessories business that made his fortune.

'My idea is to have nothing left. Absolutely nothing,' he told the *Daily Telegraph*. 'Money is counterproductive – it prevents happiness.' Instead, he would move out of his luxury Alpine retreat into a small wooden hut in the mountains or a simple bedsit in Innsbruck. His entire proceeds were going to charities he set up in Central and Latin America.

'For a long time I believed that more wealth and luxury automati-
cally meant more happiness,' he said. 'But more and more I heard the
words: "Stop what you are doing now – all this luxury and consumer-
ism – and start your real life." I had the feeling I was working as a
slave for things that I did not wish for or need.'

Mr Rabeder made his monumental decision while he was on holiday in Hawaii. 'It was the biggest shock in my life, when I realized
how horrible, soulless and without feeling the five-star lifestyle is,' he
said. 'In those three weeks, we spent all the money you could possibly
spend. But in all that time, we had the feeling we hadn't met a single
real person – that we were all just actors. The staff played the role of
being friendly and the guests played the role of being important and
nobody was real.' Since selling his belongings, Mr Rabeder said he
felt 'free, the opposite of heavy'.

So often we assume that as we get older life becomes ordered
and settled and the need for change lessens. We believe that
being grown up is about acquiring wealth and status and
having set attitudes and opinions when in reality this is a stag-
nant and unfulfilling way to live. Our angels don't want us to
live this way. They want us to keep changing and growing
and to keep questioning our motives and our attitudes. They
want us to do this because they know that the more we question, the more we open our minds, the more chance we have
of coming to a new understanding of ourselves and seeing our
angels.

Two ways to see the world

Our angels want nothing more than for us to experience the joy and love of living in the light, and, to help nudge us in the right direction, every now and again they will send us those 'thunderbolts and lightning' inspirations, when for a few brief moments we catch a glimpse of the divine and understand what is truly meaningful in our lives.

When these moments happen we have two clear choices. We can distrust or ignore them, or we can see them for the miracles that they are. I always remember the moment when I was a teenager reading something that Albert Einstein said: 'There are two ways to see the world. Either you can expect nothing to be a miracle or you can expect everything to be a miracle.' Einstein seemed to indicate that the latter is the preferable approach to life.

When I was a teenager I didn't really understand this. I thought that it was a fine thing for Einstein to say, because miracles probably come a lot easier if you have the mind of a genius. Not being a genius myself, I just couldn't relate to it. However, ever since angels started to reveal themselves to me, I have found myself referencing this quote time and time again, because it sums up so brilliantly what I am trying to get across in my writing and especially in this book. What Einstein is really saying here is that however much scientists try to explain the world rationally, we should never lose our attitude of mystery and awe. We should never forget that life itself is a miracle that can't be explained. We should never forget that life is full of wonder and unexplained mysteries.

As I've described in this book and my previous angel books, I have been through some very dark, tough and lonely times in my life but also some miraculous changes. All this has taught me that you can't ever predict what is going to happen in your life. You may think the future is written, but then something or someone comes along and you are left with a blank page to start all over again.

Just as the pages of your life get rewritten, the map of the world is also constantly redrawn. For instance, while I'm writing this chapter a cloud of volcanic ash has suspended all flights across the UK for close to a week. Holidaymakers, businesses, industries and so on have all been thrown into chaos but amid that chaos and confusion there is also the unprecedented opportunity to look up and enjoy the clear, blue skies. It's the same with your life – you think you will never fall in love again and then you sit down next to someone on the bus you have an instant connection with. You think you've got it made and then the bank holding your money collapses and you have to start all over again. Things change all the time.

The most unproductive and unfulfilling thing you can do is resist or ignore change. You have to be prepared for it. You have to live your life as though it could change at any moment, because as the stories in this chapter have shown, it really could. You have to appreciate what you already have, in case things shift and you lose something or someone important to you, but you also have to be prepared to let go of the past and move forward to a new way of living.

In the words of Einstein, and your angels, you have to treat each moment of your life with an attitude of awe, gratitude and mystery.

CHAPTER 3

Heavenly Healing

*And yet when I look up to the sky, I somehow feel
that everything will change for the better, that this
cruelty too shall end, that peace and tranquillity
will return once more.*

Anne Frank

You may have heard or read about stories of heavenly healing,
when lives are healed or saved against all odds, and angelic intervention seems the only possible explanation. Stories like these
may force even the most sceptical among us to at least consider
the possibility that something not of this world is watching over
us. For the people directly involved there is no doubt that the
miraculous experience not only saved their lives but changed
them for ever.

Here's a breathtaking story of heavenly healing that caught
the headlines in recent years:

The Christmas miracle

A woman died during childbirth on Christmas Eve, 2009, and her baby was born lifeless — but then both were revived. It's been dubbed a Christmas miracle after the amazing recovery of the pair in Colorado Springs, USA.

According to medical reports, Tracy Hermanstorfer stopped breathing while she was giving birth and after minutes passed with no sign of life doctors decided to deliver her baby by Caesarean section. But the baby was lifeless too and it was thought mother and baby were both dead. However, as medical staff managed to revive the baby boy, his mother incredibly started breathing again.

Doctors say she had no heartbeat for about four minutes.

'We are both believers . . . but this right here, even a nonbeliever — you explain to me how this happened,' Mr Hermanstorfer, 37, said. 'There is no other explanation.' He described the moment when he thought his wife had died.'I was holding her hand when we realized she was gone. My entire life just rolled out.'

Dr Stephanie Martin, a specialist in maternal-foetal medicine at Memorial Hospital, said: 'She had no signs of life. No heartbeat, no blood pressure, she wasn't breathing.'

Doctors then carried out the emergency Caesarean section to deliver their son, who has been named Coltyn. The baby boy was revived in Mr Hermanstorfer's arms and soon began to breathe.

'His life began in my hands,' the father said. 'That's a feeling like none other. Life actually began in the palm of my hands.'

No real explanation has been given for why Mrs Hermanstorfer's heart stopped and then started again. Dr Martin said it was possible that delivering the child could have restarted the heart by increasing the blood flow to the rest of her body, but it was not really clear. 'I don't have a great explanation,' she said. 'From my personal perspective, I will take help wherever I can get it.'

The mother and baby were allowed home on Monday, apparently in good health.

What do you think? Is this a miracle? For all those personally involved there is no doubt that it was.

Luke Fisher, whose story was reported in the *Worcester News* in April 2010, is also convinced that a miracle saved his life. Here's his story:

Angel tattoo saved my life

Luke Fisher, a teenager of Stalls Farm Road, Droitwich, had the guardian angel tattooed on his torso just two days before breaking his neck in three places in a car crash.

Doctors feared he might never walk again. But the eighteen-year-old has defied their predictions and looks set to make a full recovery. Mr Fisher had the guardian angel tattooed around his chest and back, with the words 'Only the strong survive' underneath it just two days before the accident.

Then there are remarkable stories of coma victims recovering, and instances of people who have been declared dead or beyond all medical help, but who go on to defy the experts and make spectacular recoveries. Such stories are beloved by the media and whenever they are reported there is always talk of divine intervention and miracles, because medical opinion has been turned on its head. This is the definition of a miracle – something that can't be explained by the laws of nature as we have defined them. A miracle is therefore both awe-inspiring and humbling because it reminds us that, even though we have advanced scientifically and medically, our understanding of the laws of life, nature and death itself is still limited, and we have underestimated the miraculous healing power of love.

The stories mentioned above were well reported by the media, but similar unpublicized ones – which are just as remarkable, but not shared with journalists for one reason or another – have been sent to me over the years. They include spontaneous healings and stories of incredible survival against all odds. The following is fairly typical – if there is such a thing as typical – of ordinary, but extraordinary, heavenly healings. Let's begin with Arnie's intriguing story:

Get the picture

I nearly died when I was thirty-three. I'd been diagnosed with colon cancer, and it had spread to my liver. Doctors gave me only six months to a year to live. Before my diagnosis I'd been an athletic young man. I played football most weekends and had several marathons under my belt. In my late twenties I did spot some of the warning signs, but I was too embarrassed to go to my doctor about problems 'down there'. I figured I just had haemorrhoids or something, but when the pain and the bleeding got so bad and I was forced to go to my doctor I found out the terrible truth. I had cancer.

When you're young – I'm in my sixties now – you think you are invincible. Death is something that happens only to other people. Faced with my own mortality I think I went into denial at first. I tried to carry on as normal, but it was impossible. I was too frail. When I was hospitalized the reality of my situation hit me. Then, perhaps inevitably, depression set in and I lost all will to survive.

Friends and family gathered around, as they do. My mother was particularly cut up. She couldn't hide her distress at all. Dad and my brothers were better at coping. As for my friends, I eventually asked the nurses to send them away. I didn't have anything to say to them and they didn't know how to behave around me. Sometimes I would wake up crying, because when I fell asleep I longed for the release of death. The nurses tried to cheer me up, keep me going, but I couldn't see any point any more.

I think you get the picture. I wasn't one of those inspiring people you read about or see on TV shows and the news who face death with dignity and courage. I was probably very much the opposite. I was angry and bitter, a nightmare to be around.

As I made it so difficult for people to be around me, I had a lot of time alone. I would just lie there, feeling wretched. It was on one of those occasions when I was by myself that I believe something incredible happened. A man came in. I'd never seen him before. He looked a bit like me, but that's about as much as I can say about him. At first I thought he was a nurse because he pottered around my room for a bit, tidying things up. Then he came up to me and sat on my bed. He looked at me for a while and then rummaged around in his pocket and took out a little silver angel figure. He handed it to me and told me to hold onto it whenever I felt all hope was lost. Then he got up and walked out.

A few moments later my regular nurse walked in and I asked her who the guy was. Surely she must have passed him on her way out. She smiled and told me to stop playing games. It was obvious who that person was. It was one of my brothers. I told her that he most certainly wasn't. She looked a little shocked and apologized. She had only let him come in to see me because she had assumed, given the likeness between us, that we were brothers.

For the rest of the day I couldn't stop thinking about this guy. It certainly took my mind off things for a while. Why would he lie like that? Why would he say he was my brother? It just didn't make sense.

Later that evening my mother noticed the silver angel on the table beside my bed. She asked me where I had got it and I told her the story about my mysterious visitor, and how my nurse had thought he was my brother because we looked so alike. Mum gasped and for a few seconds looked paler than I did. Rather uncharacteristically, when you consider how self-centred I had been these past few months, I asked her if she was OK. It was then that I got some mind-blowing news. I had a twin brother. He had died a few minutes after we were both born. My mother had never told me about him, though, because she also had been an only surviving twin. She had always known about her twin sister dying and it had been a source of much grief and longing in her life. She didn't want me to feel a similar kind of incompleteness.

From that moment on my mind had something entirely different to focus on and with that change of focus my health dramatically improved. Every time I felt sorry for myself or bad, I took the silver angel out and held it until I felt better. I also started to read books on creative visualization, healing myself by altering the way I pictured my illness in my head. I would lie there in bed imagining a battle going on in my body, between my cancer cells and the forces of light. I pictured myself strong, healthy, happy and playing football again.

As the months passed I got stronger and stronger. I stopped lying in bed all day and moved around my room to get myself a drink or a snack. I kept thinking about my twin brother and the awesome possibility that he might have returned to give me my strength back. Or perhaps as we looked so alike he didn't want me cramping his style in heaven just yet!

Seven months after the doctors gave up on me I went for my usual X-ray and my doctor looked puzzled instead of apologetic as he normally did. He went out of the room to get a second opinion. Another doctor walked in and she looked equally shocked. I asked them what was wrong and they both said in unison, 'That's what's wrong – nothing.'

Seven months ago cancer was attacking my liver and further tests confirmed that it had quite literally disappeared. My doctors asked me what was going on and I told them that I had been visualizing my body healing, with the help of my silver angel. They didn't believe me and on my medical forms it simply read – spontaneous regression, which in my mind is just another way of saying 'miracle'.

Arnie's story is amazing. There is so much going on here – a visit from his brother in spirit, the healing power of angels, and the power of mind over body – all combining forces to combat the spread of sickness. His experience brings to mind other stories of spontaneous miracle cures, such as those that have frequently been reported at the Shrine of the Virgin in Lourdes, France. Lourdes, of course, is where a spring is said to have appeared on the spot where the Virgin Mary allegedly appeared to a fourteen-year-old girl named Bernadette Soubirous in 1858. Since then millions of people have made a pilgrimage to Lourdes for miraculous healing and large numbers have claimed that they have been helped.

Continuing the life-changing heavenly healing theme of this chapter, I'd like to share a couple more hospital-based stories with you. Not surprisingly, because it is a place where emotions tend to be heightened, a large proportion of the stories sent in to me are based on hospitals. Once when I had an overnight stay in hospital I asked a group of ten or so nurses how many of them had seen an angel at some point in the hospital. Seven of them put their hands up – that's way over half.

One of the most interesting things for me, as a researcher and writer of all matters supernatural, is that hospital angel stories tend to have a higher proportion of full-blown angel sightings or encounters. In other words, these astonishing angel encounters are experienced from the outside in, rather than the inside out. Kate's story is a fine example.

Funfair

Hi. I was in hospital in August 2009 age fifty-seven for an op on my hyperthyroid. I was really scared to go under the knife but I had to have the op no matter what, so there I was in my hospital bed. My late grandmother had always told me to ask my guardian angel for help but I had never really taken this seriously before. I thought it was all nonsense.

However, on the night before my operation I did think about what Granny had said. I prayed that I would be fine and wake up after the operation. This was about two a.m. I lay awake for ages. I was just about to doze off when I got a sign from her. It wasn't directed at me but on the bed opposite. This woman's bed just lit up like a Christmas tree. There were all sorts of flashing lights running through tubes around her bed. The chart at the bottom of her bed lit up in green. It would have been spectacular if it was in a funfair, not in a hospital.

After that I slept great. But next morning I looked across to the woman's bed and there were no signs of tubes from her bed. I just felt this was a sign from my guardian angel that I was going to be OK . . . and I was.

Jacky's fascinating story also took place in a hospital – in the intensive-care unit.

The window

Five years ago I was involved in a head-on collision with another car. All I can remember is driving up a hill and then seeing this car coming straight at me. The next thing I remember is waking up in hospital, with bandages all over me. I had a severe head injury, broken ribs, a broken leg and third-degree burns over 25 per cent of my body. Worse still – because I was a piano teacher – both my wrists were broken and the fingers on my right hand were crushed. There was talk of having it removed. I would never play the piano again.

My brother told me that a drunk driver had caused the accident. He'd died on impact and I was lucky to be alive. It certainly didn't feel that way for me. I'd lost everything – my music, my health and my looks. I didn't have anything left to live for. The pain and discomfort I was in were unbearable. I couldn't imagine it would get any better and even if it did I would live with scars for the rest of my life. At times I wished the driver had finished us both off.

About three weeks after my collision I was still in intensive care. My head injury – the immediate cause for concern – was stabilizing, but my vision was still poor. Doctors made it clear to me that my recovery would be a slow one. My brother offered to take care of me – we lost our mum and dad when we were little – but I could tell it was causing strain for him. You see, he'd recently got married and had a baby on the way. It didn't seem fair for them to be looking after me at what should be such a happy time in their lives. I felt like a burden.

One evening I told my brother that I didn't want him to take care of me. I lied and told him that I didn't really like his wife – which isn't true, I just said that to make him angry. It worked. He got very upset and left saying he wouldn't bother coming back if I felt that way. When he had gone, I felt terrible. I'd sent him away because I didn't want to be a burden to him, but this didn't give me much comfort. I felt so alone. Everything and everyone I loved had now gone. I remember calling out loud, 'If there is anyone out there, please let me know.'

At that instant a ray of sunlight shone across my pillow. It felt so warm and comforting and it gave me such a sense of peace. I have very few memories of my mum, but I do remember her picking me up once when I fell over and cuddling me. The ray of sunlight was giving me the same feeling. It stayed with me for several hours until I drifted off to sleep. It was such a simple thing, a shaft of sunlight from a window, but it meant the world to me.

The following morning my brother's wife came to see me. She told me off for upsetting my brother so much because she knew how close we were to each other. She also told me that being a woman herself she knew exactly what I was doing. I didn't want to be a burden, but I hadn't asked them what they wanted and what they wanted was to pull together as a family.

After I was eventually released from hospital, I surprised doctors with the speed of my recovery. Apart from a few scars, if you saw me today you wouldn't really be able to tell. I have stopped teaching piano but music is still very much a part of my life, and I train local choirs. I stayed at my brother's for close to a year, but now I'm busy living my own life again.

I told my brother and his wife about the ray of sunlight and how it had comforted me and given me strength and hope on that terrible night I had tried to send my brother away. They both looked very confused when I told them because I had been in intensive care and there had been no windows!

Although in some cases alternative explanations for spontaneous miracle cures, like those that occur at Lourdes, have been found, in many more cases the experts simply can't explain how or why someone is cured. However, in an encouraging sign that the medical profession is moving forward, most doctors today would freely admit that a change in the patient's thinking, such as belief in divine grace, could bring about a cure. I have no doubt that medical opinion is right in this instance, and those who are healed do change their thinking and adjust their outlooks and their lifestyles in ways that cultivate inner peace. I also have no doubt that true healing begins from the inside out, from the angel within us.

The healing power of thoughts

Moving on with the theme of healing from the inside out, it seems clear that our thoughts can have a powerful effect on our health and our lives. As mentioned above, few doctors would disagree with this, as all too often they have seen how people recover and heal faster when they believe they can be healed. Yet, as far as most investigators are concerned if a healing is to be regarded as miraculous or of divine origin, it must be demonstrated that something occurred that could not be accounted for by the patient's positive thinking alone.

Those who believe need no proof of the power of positive thought – or prayer – but for those who want hard evidence one place to look is what happens when sick people are prayed for without their knowledge.

Indeed, there have been many scientific studies investigating the power of prayer. In 1999 a study at Duke University Medical Center entitled, 'A Randomized, Controlled Trial of the Effects of Remote, Intercessory Prayer on Outcomes in Patients admitted to the Coronary Care Unit' (Archives of

Internal Medicine, October, 1999, 159, 2273-78) indicated that those patients being prayed for without their knowledge had the lowest rate of complications of any of the other groups. Here, the placebo-effect argument (people get well because of positive expectation) can't explain the fact that prayed-for patients were significantly improved when compared to other patients.

Other more recent studies conducted around the world have shown the healing effects of prayer. People of faith believe that angels directly intervene to heal or save lives and perhaps even the most secular-minded can see how prayer might work. If, as modern science believes, all matter and life consists of units of energy – including our thoughts – then it is feasible that through a concentration of thought in prayer, this energy can be directed to achieve or influence the health and wellbeing of others.

Sure, you could call this the power of positive expectation, rather than the power of prayer, but whatever you call it, it really does seem to work – to have real effects on people's lives. Sandra certainly believes that her father's life was touched by the miracle of answered prayers. Here's her story.

Travel in peace

I thought you would be interested in something that happened to me earlier in the year, when we were on holiday in Arizona.

During our last few days there I received a message from my daughter. My dad had been ill while we were away. She hadn't wanted to tell me while I was on holiday, but his condition had deteriorated and he was in a critical condition

We couldn't get back to the airport any sooner than we had planned and I was very concerned that he would pass away before we got home and I wanted to be with my mother. I prayed very hard that day; I called for the angels to go to him and I imagined them around him healing and encouraging him. As we were driving I looked up to see a signpost that read, 'Travel in peace'; some miles along another sign appeared and two words jumped out at me: 'Guardian Angel'.

After many prayers and Hail Marys I slept better than I had thought I would. The next day I had a message from my daughter to say that Dad had against all odds 'pulled himself around'. He was even trying to sit up and read the paper! I'm sure you know that in the States any kind of numberplate is allowed as long as it doesn't offend or clash with another. The next day as we were travelling my husband drew my attention to a car we were passing. It was an old pink cadillac with a sweet-looking old man driving. His numberplate was 'Hail Mary'.

This sounds very fanciful but both my husband and the friend travelling with us saw it. I felt the tension drain from me as I just knew Dad was being looked after. He's back home now — he still struggles with poor health, but we'll have him a while longer.

Judy sent me this wonderful story about her mother.

Praying hands

My brilliant mum — who has since passed away — told me this story. She was the most honest and straight person anyone could meet. I know it is true.

66

It was 1972 and my mum had been in hospital for several months. What started out as a simple hysterectomy had turned into an infection that was literally draining the life out of her body. The doctors didn't know what caused it, but she got weaker and weaker and lost weight rapidly. There's so much talk about hospital-based infections these days and I suspect she might have fallen victim to one of those, but back then there wasn't as much awareness as there is today. At one point Mum weighed less than seven stone and she had always been a really well-built woman. She couldn't keep any of her food down and was placed on drips. This went on for a few more months. Mum lost more weight and my dad was told that doctors thought Mum would die.

My mum was not a woman of faith. In her youth I know she had been drawn to the Church, but I think she got disillusioned over the years. She loved to collect photographs of religious and spiritual art, though, and her favourite was a painting called 'The Praying Hands'. If you haven't seen it, it's an exquisitely drawn picture of a pair of hands raised in prayer. One day when my dad came to visit her she asked him to bring that print in because she said it always comforted her. My dad brought the picture in and placed it by her bedside. For the rest of the day my mum and dad stared at it, both praying for a miracle. She didn't want to die, because she still had children and a husband who needed her.

The next morning doctors began to make incisions to try to drain the infection. It was their last resort and the chances of success were slim. All through the day the infection poured out of my mum — everything came out. By the evening my mum was craving solid food for the first time in four months. She had survived.

I truly believe that the prayers of my mum and dad in the hospital that day worked a miracle. I truly believe that angels are all around us. I hope you use my story. I'd like others to know about it.

Sarah also believes that healing prayers and thoughts have worked a miracle.

Healing hands

How do I start? I have had uncontrolled epilepsy all my life, and over the course of my life I have tried eleven different types of anti-convulsant pills with no success. Fifteen years ago, I had an operation on my temporal lobe and that helped ease the condition a little but it still was there. That's when I tried Chinese acupuncture. It helped and my medication was decreased but I was still not much better, so through my life I have always lived with an uncontrolled monster.

Three years ago I suffered a breakdown while I was in hospital. I had the most magic moment. It felt as if something special was with me. It didn't last long enough, though, to sustain me long-term and by the beginning of this year I was at the end of the line again. Then another magical thing happened. I began to feel better, and it's all down to a wonderful spiritual healer called Dorothy Wilson who prays for me. Whenever I visit her or think about her I feel calm and in control of my life and not afraid of having seizures any more. I'm a different person. I'm not alone with this any more.

Emma, who is thirteen years old, sent me this delightful angel story to share.

Wonderful miracle

Every year I go to my auntie's house for two weeks in the summer. I have a great time there, playing in their huge garden, bouncing on the trampoline, and feeding the horses. Then one day, when I was outside soaking up the sun with my cousins, my auntie came out with some sad news. Her friend's little boy called Ben, who was only about three years old, got this terrible, serious illness (I can't remember what it's called), where his neck is in a completely strange position, nearly back-to-front, and he can't move it. I have never met this boy Ben, but I felt so sorry for him.

Later on that day, we all decided that we should pray for this little boy. And so we did. Every day for a full week we all sat down in a group and said our prayers. After that week we got a phone call from Ben's mum saying that Ben could now move his neck freely and was extremely happy. The doctors and nurses couldn't believe it! They can only describe it as a miracle! I truly believe our prayers were answered, and Ben's guardian angel was watching over him.

I wrote back to Emma to tell her that I believed her sincere prayers did help heal Ben. From all that I have read and learned over the years about this kind of phenomenon it seems that the prayers of people who have confidence that miracles are always possible are exceptionally powerful. In times past we would call people like these healers or miracle workers. I prefer to call them aspiring angels, because of their conviction that every-thing is going to be all right, despite every depressing thing they know about the situation.

We can all be aspiring angels by cultivating a similar attitude of inner peace that facilitates healing in both others and ourselves. And recognizing that sometimes there are times when we can't do anything except pray for divine guidance is the best place to start.

But what exactly is prayer?

Prayer is a word I was initially reluctant to use because for many people it is so closely associated with religion – and to risk repeating myself, angels are non-denominational. There is no doubt – and certainly nothing wrong with the fact – that many people do find great comfort and strength from traditional forms of prayer. But for those of us who are unfamiliar or uncomfortable with such things, prayer is simply a way of communicating with our angels. Your thoughts are a form of prayer, and because your angels are always listening to what goes on in your mind and your heart, your thoughts have great power.

Maggie was astonished by the power of her silent thoughts. Here's her story.

New hope

Back in 1991, my husband Stan was undergoing a very serious operation. None of the doctors told me directly, but I knew that they didn't hold out much hope for him. It was a very long operation and I was advised to go home and they would contact me when there was news. I didn't want to leave the hospital but my sister made me. Now, I've never been the religious sort. Church wasn't a place for me, but when I got home I prayed with all my heart that God would guide the surgeon's hand so that Stan would pull through. I just sat there quietly in my living room, with a cup of tea in my hand and love for Stan in my heart. I had no idea how I would go on without him.

An agonizing four hours later I got the call from the hospital and heard the words I had longed to hear. Stan had made it. He had pulled through. I rushed to the hospital and spent most of the next few weeks there by his side as he went from strength to strength.

Anyway, here's the most incredible but brilliant part of my story. A few days after Stan's surgery when the surgeon came down to see me and Stan he said something that took my breath away. He told me that it really had been touch-and-go at the beginning, and at one point they were going to abandon the operation, but then he suddenly got the strength and focus to complete it. He said that out of nowhere he just knew what he had to do. He even used the words, 'It was as if something was guiding my hands.'

I told him about my silent prayers and he just smiled. I didn't press it any further as I didn't want him to think I was saying that he couldn't have done it without some help from above, because he was a brilliant surgeon, but inside I knew that my prayers had been answered. For the first time in my life, I believed in something. For the first time I felt a surge of joy and hope.

Stan passed on in 1999, so we got another nine years together. I'm so grateful for that time. It meant the world to me. I miss him deeply, but whenever I feel that he has gone, I sit quietly and think about him and he is all around me again. Don't ask me how, but I know he hasn't died. I know he is out there somewhere. I don't tell many people about my beliefs, because I don't think they would understand me, but something tells me you will understand my letter.

Have you ever felt a surge of energy or warmth when someone says that you are in their prayers, or that they are thinking of you?

Turning to prayer, sending positive thoughts and seeking divine guidance and help in times of need, whether for yourself or others, is often considered to be the last resort, but based on all that I have read and myself experienced over the years about the power of prayer to heal lives, I firmly believe it should be the first resort. Remember, you don't need to go down on your knees to pray, you don't even need to say anything out loud. Prayer is just another word for thought – thought that is intense, concentrated and, above all, heartfelt.

As Olivia's story shows it seems that heartfelt thought can truly move mountains.

A day like no other

Two years ago this March, I was driving to work. As usual I had my radio playing and I was gathering my thoughts for the day ahead. It was basically a very ordinary day. I'd been driving for about forty minutes when I saw a cyclist ahead of me. He was pedalling furiously and was clearly quite a professional as he had one of those speed bikes. As I passed him I noticed that he wasn't wearing a helmet and I felt myself getting angry and concerned that he should be putting his life at risk in this way. It was a busy road and the visibility wasn't that great.

I'd already driven past the cyclist when out of nowhere a car came round a corner at great speed and on the wrong side of the road. It sounds like a cliché but my life flashed before me. I was convinced we were going to smash into each other and screamed out loud for help. I wanted to try to swerve but a voice told me to hit my brakes. The voice was so clear and authoritative that I hit my brakes.

I was sure that this was it and that if there was an afterlife I was going to find out, but when I opened my eyes the car had swerved past me. I was sitting in my car, stopped neatly on the side of the road, and I was completely unhurt. Police cars flashed passed me in hot pursuit of what was obviously a stolen vehicle. I got out of my car, feeling shaken by it all, and as I did I saw in the distance the speeding car crash into a tree and spin around in the middle of the road, taking out the cyclist I had passed earlier. I felt sick and just stood by my car crying. There was no way that guy was going to live – he didn't even have his helmet on.

I dried my eyes and phoned for an ambulance. Then I drove hesitantly to the scene to see if I could help. When I got there I saw something incredible – my cyclist was standing there shaking and he had his helmet on! Is it possible that my thoughts had somehow influenced him and made him stop and put his helmet on? I'll never know because I never got the chance to ask him – by now other people had arrived on the scene to help – but all in all it was a day like no other for me.

Olivia's story is a fantastic example of intense prayer not just for her own life, but also sincere heartfelt concern for another. Mary's story, below, also shows that sometimes our angels will respond to our silent prayers, those thoughts we don't even realize we are thinking.

Growing up

I hope you like my story. It's one I really want to share with others because I think it will give them lots to think about — it still gives me tingles down my spine just writing it down for you.

Last year I was not in a good place at all. My second marriage had failed and I was raising my three kids, from two different fathers, virtually alone. Both my marriages had been disasters from start to finish really. I should have known better but I couldn't help myself. I just seemed to attract men who weren't good news. My first husband slept with my best friend in the first year of our marriage and my second husband couldn't keep it in his trousers either. I felt lonely and depressed and didn't really know where to turn.

What I understand now is that growing up without a father had had a huge impact on my relationships with men. On the outside I looked like a confident person but deep down I always felt that I wasn't worthy of a man's love. I remember my mum telling me that my dad had walked out when I was born. She told me that being a dad was too much for him. Sometimes I think she blamed me. I've always had a complicated relationship with my mum. I remember trying to get to sleep at night and hearing her arguing with her latest boyfriend. They never stuck around long either and each time one left, she blamed me. On top of all this we were constantly on the move. Mum could never stay in one place for more than a year or two.

Unhappy living with Mum, I left home as soon as I could and when I was sixteen I got a job as a waitress and really enjoyed the independence of taking care of myself. I did my job so well that within a year I was put in charge of all the other girls and five years down the line, the manager of the restaurant chain put me forward for management training. My career took off but my private life nosedived. Not only did I have girlfriends I couldn't trust, I chose boyfriends that weren't good for me. I didn't have good role models of a loving father and mother and no one to show me how relationships should work. I didn't wish for it to be any other way because I had no idea things could be any different. I just thought all relationships were like this.

Fast-forwarding to my second divorce, I was sitting alone in my room one day feeling pretty sorry for myself. I started daydreaming about winning the lottery when suddenly, out of nowhere, I was filled with this compulsion to find my father. I'd never been interested in him before, so I don't know where it came from.

I got in touch with my mum and told her I needed to talk to get in touch with my father because I had to fill out a medical form. Then she told me something that made everything in my head spin into chaos. My father was dead. He had died a few months before my second birthday. When I pressed my mum for more details she started to sob and told me that he died saving my life. There had been a fire in the family home. My dad managed to save me by wrapping me up in wet towels but the smoke inhalation had killed him. I asked Mum why she had never told me and she said it was because my screaming had made him go back into the building. He had been the love of her life, and try as hard as she could, she could never really forgive me for that.

After that highly charged phone call I felt as if I had been hit in the stomach. My mother still blamed me for my father's absence, but it wasn't for the reason I had always thought. What I had learned

– and what gave me a feeling of warmth, comfort and strength I had never known before – was that my father had loved me so much he had laid down his life for me. I hadn't been the mistake Mum had always made me feel I was. I had been wanted and I had been loved, fiercely loved. Just knowing that has turned my life around. I've ditched my toxic friends and have given myself a bit of a life makeover. I feel like a new person. I thought I would never say this, but I actually like myself. Sadly, Mum and I still haven't fully worked things out, but perhaps in time.

If I ever get into a relationship again, it will be with someone who treats me right and if I never have a relationship again the love my father had for me will inspire me to love myself with the same passion. I will teach my kids to have confidence and self-respect. I will let them know that they are loved and that they are worthy of being loved.

Sonia's angels also listened to her silent, unspoken prayers for comfort and direction following the departure of her husband.

A freedom I have never known

I read and very much enjoyed your book – *An Angel Healed Me* – and when I had finished it, I knew that I had to write to you with my experience. It's still very fresh in my mind as it only happened two years ago, when I was seventy-five.

My seventy-sixth year was both the worst and the best year of my life. I'll try to explain what I mean. It was the worst because I lost my husband of forty years. We'd met at school and our lives had been intertwined ever since. He did everything for me and I took care of him and our five children. When he died I felt like I had lost half of myself. I didn't know who I was. My kids had long since left the nest and didn't need me any more. The love of my life had gone and I was all alone. Simple things like changing light bulbs, paying the bills or reading electricity meters defeated me, because he'd always seen to those.

I didn't have any friends to fall back on either. Ours had been such a happy marriage we never needed anyone else. I had always thought I would die before him because he was so much fitter and stronger, but cancer took him from me. So there I was, alive but scared to live without my other half and not knowing where to turn.

After the funeral I considered travelling to Switzerland, to end it all. I didn't tell any of my kids because I knew they would try to talk me out of it, but it seemed the only solution. I got all the necessary forms and started to quietly make preparations. That was me – you see – always the quiet one, never making a fuss.

Then one day as I was coming back from the local shops with some milk and bread and other items I felt this quick, intense pain in my chest. It was over before it began so I didn't think anything of it, just something we old people have to put up with, but that night when I was in bed it struck again. It felt as if a fist was squeezing my heart. I couldn't breathe. It was as I lay there in pain, uncertain if this was my end or not, that I became aware of a figure in my room.

I was awake, and although the appearance of the figure was unusual it didn't scare me. At first I thought it was my husband, but it looked like my father and my mother as well. Wrapped around it was a swirling mist of yellow. I could not take my eyes off the figure.

I was spellbound and then I heard a voice. I recognized the voice, but I couldn't quite decide who it was, and the voice told me it was time to 'begin again'. I squinted and looked at the figure again and this time I recognized who it was. It was me, only me when I was about eighteen years old, just before I met my husband. I looked so confident, strong and happy. As soon as I recognized myself the vision faded, and the pain in my heart disappeared.

The next morning the most astonishing thing happened. I wasn't crying. I wasn't unhappy. I wanted to get up and start a new day. I wanted to spend time with my grandchildren. I wanted to hear the birds sing. I wanted to sort my finances out. I wanted to buy a cat. I've always loved cats, but when I was growing up we couldn't afford one and when I was married my husband was allergic so I'd never been able to have one. Now, with it just being me, I could have one at last.

Don't get me wrong – I still miss my husband with every heartbeat, but my vision had shown me that it was time to take back the part of myself I had given away to him. It was time for me to lavish some love and attention on myself. Wherever he was, I knew that this was what my husband would have wanted me to do. We had had such a happy life together, and throwing away my chance at life would not have honoured his memory. I tore up the Switzerland-clinic forms and as I did I had this overwhelming sense that my husband was resting his hand on my shoulder. My spirit felt like it was being bathed in love.

Today, I'm still not very outgoing. Often it's just me and my three rescue cats, but I do open up more to the people I love and who love me. I don't hide who I am any more and I'm not afraid to ask for help if I need it, or talk to strangers. Living like this, opening myself up to the world around me, is a freedom I have never known before.

My youngest daughter – who believes in angels – is convinced that I saw an angel that night and that I had a spiritual experience. I don't know what I had but it was something so powerful and profound. My doctor checked for signs of a stroke but there was nothing. I did want to tell him about my healing vision, but when you get to my age you've got to be careful when you start talking to doctors about hearing voices! So it remains a secret for me, my daughter and now you and I hope all the people who read this story. If it was my angel, touching my life with a vision, then I can only think I was being shown the person I could still be. I was being shown that whatever age you are, and however many people you lose, life is still a precious and wonderful thing.

Your angels know your heart better than you do, and sometimes you don't need to articulate your hidden needs for them to reach out to you. All you need to do to hear and see them is slow down, sit quietly and reflect. As you'll read in John's account, it is during such times of quiet reflection that life-changing spiritual experiences can happen.

Wide awake

I'm a bit of a worrier and every night before I go to sleep I always spend some time fretting about my day, thinking how I could have done things better or if I have made the right decisions in my work and private life. I'm emailing you because last night as I was just about to fall asleep I felt this warm glow. I opened my eyes and there were lights all around my body. I felt completely relaxed, it wasn't scary. Then I felt myself float a few inches above my body. I don't know how I did that because I was lying under my blankets – it was like I passed through the blankets. Anyway, as I floated I saw this blinding white light. It was like nothing I have ever seen on earth. It was lifting me up and it was all around me and within me. I could go on and on using so many different words to describe it but at the end of the day it was indescribable.

When I woke up the next morning, it was bright and early. A good two hours before my alarm went off at six a.m. I was wide awake so I decided to get up and go over some of my work to check it was right. As I put the kettle on, though, I realized that there was no need to go over my work. I had double-checked it the day before. Letting go of the worry was incredible for me. All day it was the same. I left the house without checking dozens of times if I had switched things off or locked the door. At work I did everything to the best of my ability and then stopped fretting about it. In the evening I played with my kids and hugged my wife without worrying that I had more 'important' things to do. And when I went to bed, I thought of sunny beaches and recalled all the laughter in the day, instead of all the things that had gone wrong.

Since my 'light' experience I can honestly say that I am not a worrier any more. It was as if overnight I realized that worry is a completely useless thing to do – it won't change anything or do anything. All it did was make me anxious. I have not worried about any decision I have made since, as I just trust myself. Do you think I had a spiritual experience?

I wrote back to John to tell him that he most certainly had a spiritual experience and he should rejoice in it. I told him that I have received letters from many other people telling me that they have had similar unusual sensations or had a moment of understanding or revelation during prayer or quiet reflection. I'm not taking about meditation here, or complicated rituals for invoking angels. You don't need to learn any techniques to connect with your angels. You just need an open mind and a heartfelt desire to understand the truth and meaning of your life.

Without a doubt people's lives do seem to change after prayer or heartfelt thought. There is a flash of recognition, a fleeting glimpse of divine truth that illuminates an entire lifetime. A moment when we just sense, feel or know something we did not know, when a thought, a feeling triggers a connection with the divine.

Perhaps at this point you are still thinking to yourself: Why hasn't something like this ever happened to me? Why can't I have such a life-enhancing experience? As you read on, I'd like to ask you to hold this thought in your head, and I'm gently warning you, it's an incredibly powerful thought that may trigger all sorts of astonishing experiences, and that thought is: Perhaps I already have.

Dig deep into your heart and perhaps you will find an echo of something that you might have missed before. Perhaps this something came in a dream, in the wise words of someone else, or in a surge of hope, love, elation or a sense of deep and true knowing in the depths of despair? Perhaps it came but you didn't recognize it at the time. Perhaps it is with you now as you read this book.

And perhaps by remembering and reconnecting with it here and now, or anticipating it in your future, it can transform into one of the defining moments of your lifetime – the first of many defining moments in your past, present and future, when 'something' becomes everything.

CHAPTER 4

Lights in the Darkness

We shall find peace.
We shall hear the angels,
We shall see the sky sparkling with diamonds.

John Milton

Of course, you could argue that angel visions and encounters are simply wishful thinking or products of an overactive imagination, but let me assure you that to all the people who experienced them and sent me their stories – and I have no reason to doubt their integrity – they were real. They know what they saw and what they saw healed not just their bodies, but their minds and their hearts, by filling them with a miraculous sense of wonder, hope and purpose, often when they thought all hope was lost.

In this chapter you'll read lots of incredible stories about angels intervening and bringing spontaneous joy into people's lives during times of intense darkness, crisis or trauma. This first astonishing story comes from America. It has been well documented, but I always feel inspired when reading it and hope you will as well.

The birdies

On 22 July 1993 Lloyd Glenn received devastating news. He was informed that his three-year-old son, Brian, had been trapped at home underneath his family's automatic garage door for several minutes, and that when his wife found him he was dead. The garage door had completely closed on his little sternum right over his heart.

Despite the severity of his injuries Brian was miraculously revived by CPR and hospital personnel, but the complete story of his miracle didn't end there. About a month after the accident Brian awake from his afternoon nap and said, 'Sit down, Mommy. I have something to tell you.

'Do you remember when I got stuck under the garage door? Well, it was so heavy and it hurt really bad. I called out to you, but you couldn't hear me. I started to cry, but then it hurt too bad. And then the birdies came.'

Brian's mother pressed him to describe the birdies in more detail. He went on to describe them as 'beautiful', dressed in white with large wings. She soon realized that he did not have the vocabulary yet to say 'angels' and was describing them as birdies because they had wings and were flying.

'The birdies made a whooshing sound and flew into the garage. They took care of me. They did. Yes, they did,' he said. 'One of the birdies came to get you. She came to tell you I got stuck under a door.'

Brian went on to describe his accident and his mother's actions and words when she found him unconscious in perfect detail. She knew there was no way that he could have been conscious during that time and guessed that his spirit must have somehow left his body and watched the scene unfold.

Brian also told his mother about a trip the birdies had taken him on. The trip was to a faraway, pretty place but the birdies told him it was time for him to go back. A bright and warm light appeared. He loved the light. Something inside it appeared and wrapped its arms around him saying he was loved, but he had to go back and tell everyone about the birdies.

In the months ahead many more people heard Brian's story and were confounded by this young child having such a detailed vocabulary at such a young age. His parents said that since that day they have never felt the same about life and death. Everything in their life feels different, brighter and newer.

Similar stories of experiencing bright lights, the rush of wings and a feeling of warmth when a person is close to death, or actually dead, but then returns to life are regularly reported all over the globe. On the very day (Monday 19 April 2010) I was writing up Brian's story for this chapter, I opened the papers and the first story to catch my eye was this one. The similarities are astonishing, I'm sure you will agree.

A lot of light

A boy of three claims he saw his great-grandmother in heaven while he was clinically dead after falling into a pond. Paul Ericke from Berlin came back to life more than three hours after his heart stopped beating. It is believed he was in the pond at his grandparents' house for several minutes before his grandmother saw him and pulled him out. His father gave him mouth-to-mouth and heart massage during the ten minutes it took the helicopter to arrive. Paramedics then took over and he was taken to hospital. Doctors tried to resuscitate him for hours. They had almost given up when three hours and eighteen minutes after he had been brought in, his heart started beating independently.

Paul's recovery astonished the medical team treating him because it is highly unusual for children who have been underwater for more than a few minutes to pull through without any sign of brain damage, as was the case for Paul. Even more extraordinary, however, was that the boy said that when he was unconscious he saw his great-grandmother Emmi, who had turned him back from a gate and urged him to go back to his parents.

Paul said, 'There was a lot of light and I was floating. I came to a gate and Grandma Emmi was on the other side. She said to me, "What are you doing here, Paul? You must go back to Mummy and Daddy. I will wait for you here." I knew I was in heaven. Heaven looked nice. But I am glad I am back with Mummy and Daddy now.'

These two stories fall into the category of near-death experiences – which we'll return to in Chapter Seven – but I feel they belong here in this chapter because they show how during times of trauma and tragedy – and nothing can be more tragic than the death of a child – beings of light are never far away. Both children were far too young to have absorbed or understood concepts of the afterlife, which makes their testimonies so very compelling. In their narrative they both mentioned sources of bright, warm and loving light. Light is also a theme in this story sent to me by Nancy a few years ago.

Bright eyes

In the winter of 2005 each night before I went to sleep I would close my eyes and immediately see points of bright lights. It was a bit like when you have been staring into a candle or looking at the sun for too long and then you close your eyes and see wonderful things. The thing is, though, I hadn't been staring at any bright lights before I went to sleep, but they were always there. I never felt frightened of the lights. They made me feel warm and cosy. Then one night I started to see figures in the centre of the lights, very tiny figures but figures all the same. And then in time the figures turned into faces, the tiny faces of loved ones who have passed on.

In March 2006 I was diagnosed with ovarian cancer, fourth stage. Doctors told me that I might not pull through. I was immediately put on a course of treatment. At night the smiling bright faces I saw gave me a lot of comfort. I thought they were preparing me for the inevitable, but then after five weeks of treatment I went to sleep for the first time without seeing them. It broke my heart. I missed them terribly. Three weeks went by with no bright faces or light, and then I understood why. Doctors gave me the all clear. The treatments were working and my tumours had shrunk miraculously.

For the past two years I have been cancer-free. To date I have not seen the bright lights again.

Visions of bright lights and angels tend to be reported more frequently when people are close to physical death or their lives are in danger. However, as these next stories show, you don't need to be close to physical death to see angels. They can, as Sherry tells us below, also appear when it feels like the spirit and heart inside you is dying.

A changed life

I was a young girl, very young, when I 'chose' to have an abortion. I had been dating a boy for the past year and we intended to get married if I got pregnant. I thought I had everything planned out so when I got pregnant I was so excited. Then bit by bit my world fell apart. Everybody started to give me their opinion and being young and unsure of myself I started to think that I had no other option and that it was the best thing for me. Everyone said I deserved to be a normal teenager and it would be better if I postponed motherhood until I had established myself in a career and my circumstances in life were better. Naively, I went along with everything I was told. It's too painful for me to go into details here but needless to say I was not prepared emotionally, spiritually or physically for what happened. As soon as I had had the abortion I felt like I had killed my baby.

I tried so hard to move on with my life. I tried to hide the feelings of guilt, shame and relief – yes, I'm honest enough to admit that relief was there as I really wasn't ready for the responsibility of a child – but I couldn't return to my life as it was before I got pregnant because my life had changed. They say time heals all wounds but time went by and try as I might to lead a normal life

I just couldn't. My baby was dead because of me. I talked to my boyfriend and to my sister but 'Get over it and move on' is all I heard anyone say. The logical reasons for my decision – the fact that I was young, didn't have a job or a home of my own – were all we discussed. Nobody wanted to talk about the emotional and spiritual scars I'd been left with. I thought constantly about death and was plagued with questions about my baby. Had I sent him or her to hell?

Six years later I was still searching for someone who would understand and help me and this is when I met my guardian angel. What I describe now came to me as a kind of vision or dream. I am not going to try to prove its validity to anyone. For me it's enough that it was real to me and that it gave me a tremendous sense of release and healing. It's hard to put down in words as it was more a feeling than anything else but here's what I sensed.

Somehow I had managed to get through university and get my first job. I did what everyone thought I should do to move forward with my life but every night after work I went home feeling empty. I went to work. I came home. I went to bed and dreamed of my dead child. Sometimes I didn't think I should exist because a part of me – my child – didn't exist any more. My self-hatred was swallowing up my life – eating me alive. Waves of guilt washed over me. There was no hope in my life.

One night I fell into bed and began to relive the whole abortion again. The pain and anguish seemed more acute than ever. I began to cry as I had done for many years but this time I began to pray for help. A part of me felt I didn't deserve help because I had murdered my baby but mercifully the stronger and better part of me prayed for strength and hope. Blinded with tears, and feeling pain like a vice in my chest, I prayed as I have never prayed before.

I'm not sure if I fell asleep or not but what I do know is that a warmth came over me and when I looked up I saw bright stars in my bedroom. The pain and anguish melted away as I saw an angel holding a baby in his arms. I couldn't see much of his face as his hair was long and each time his wings beat together his hair flew in front of his face. Then I heard him say, 'This is your child. She is with us now and she has always been with us.' I found myself wondering what the child's name was and before I could ask, the answer came – her name was Grace.

Since my vision I have found a perspective that has helped me think about the whole event and even talk to others honestly about the feelings of pain and shame inside me. I don't think the regret will ever go away but I stopped suffering from bouts of self-hatred, guilt and depression. I started to feel human again, full of love and hope that I can share with others. It took me close to fifteen years to heal the pain. The experience changed my life for ever and gave me a strength and inner peace and courage I didn't know I could have.

Abortion is a deeply painful subject. All those who have been in touch with me about it have expressed their sadness, their sense of loss, regret and guilt, which at times threatens to overshadow their chances of happiness. They also wonder if their baby suffers in the afterlife, but Sherry's story shows that when abortion takes place the spirit of that child returns to heaven. Her story also shows that however distressing, abortions can help a mother grow spiritually and emotionally, and there is always light in the darkness.

In this story below, Liam also describes how angels lifted him up at a time in his life when he desperately needed guidance.

A changed man

I've told only my closest friends this story. Some believe me and some do not but I know it to be real. In 2002 I found myself broke and homeless. My drug addiction was forcing me to do desperate things to get my hands on my gear. I won't go into that now, but I want you to know I sunk as low as a person could get.

I got hooked on drugs while I was a student at college. It started as harmless fun but five years down the line it became a deadly game. My parents did everything they could to help me. They sent me to rehab and to cleansing programmes. They took me in every time I messed up but I never stayed clean for more than a few months. After years of this even my family gave up on me. My mum was on antidepressants and dad unable to work because of the stress I caused them. I turned up one night at their house begging for money, as I had done many times, but this time my uncle was at the door and he told me to go away and never come back.

I stayed outside my house for hours begging and pleading to talk to Mum. Eventually she came to the door with red eyes and told me she couldn't help me any more. I was on my own from now on. I had no get-out clause. I was terrified. I needed to get my gear. I guess for the first time in my life I was completely honest with myself. I didn't know what to do. I sat down in the street and said to myself, 'I give up. If there is anything out there, take me.'

All of a sudden it felt as if something was pouring out of me through my head. The sensation was so intense I held my head in my hands but it didn't feel any different. Then I got the same sensation in my feet. I looked down at them and they looked no different to before. Then I looked up and saw this tiny bright light coming towards me. As it got closer and closer I didn't feel frightened, just curious. The next thing I know I feel something touch my heart. I don't know what it was but I definitely felt as if it was something or someone because it made me jump a bit. The place it had touched started to feel warm and that warmth spread all over me.

At that moment my mum opened the door and let me in. I literally collapsed into her arms. She helped me upstairs and tucked me into bed, just as she used to when I was a child. I drifted off into a heavy sleep. When I woke up I had lost my appetite for drugs. It really was that instant.

To this day I haven't even been tempted to take any gear again. It's a miracle, I know, because I didn't get any withdrawal symptoms. I'm convinced that an angel came to me that day. I am a changed man. I now know that there is a divine presence and my experience has drawn me closer to it. It's close to five years now since my miracle and it has given me such faith.

Liam's story is closer to the traditional description of angels or divine intervention in that he quite literally saw the light and was miraculously cured as a result. More often, though, our angels prefer to bring light and transformation and hope into our lives in subtler, less obvious ways that have deep significance only to the person involved. In other words, what other people may describe as nothing out of the usual or fairly ordinary is extraordinary to the individual. This was certainly the case for this grieving father, who didn't leave his name when he sent me this email in February 2010.

An angel held my hand

My fifteen-year-old daughter died two years ago of an undiagnosed heart defect. Her death was sudden and unexpected, within hours of her first symptoms. She was an only child and as you can imagine my wife and I took it very hard. The most difficult times were at night. One night about a month after she had passed over I got very upset and couldn't stop my tears. My wife had finally managed to go to sleep and I didn't want to wake her so I went out of our bedroom to calm down. The only place I could think of going was my daughter's room. I lay down on her bed and tried to pray but just ended up sobbing.

While I was sobbing the light in the hall suddenly went on. I got up, thinking my wife must have got up. but saw that she was still in bed sleeping. I turned the light off and it went back on again. And then I remembered how my beautiful daughter had always wanted us to keep the hall light on when she went to sleep. Right up until the age of fourteen she had been scared of the dark and having the light on comforted her. Was it possible that she was comforting me now? I can't think of any other explanation for the light going on like that.

I kept the hall light on and went back to our bedroom, feeling calmer than I had done before. As I drifted back to sleep I felt someone take hold of my hands in theirs. Again I thought it was my wife but she was still asleep. I just relaxed and enjoyed the sensation.

I have no doubt in my mind that my beautiful daughter is an angel and that she is comforting her mum and dad now, just as we used to when she suffered from her night-time fears. She always hated the dark, but about six months before she died she lost her fear completely.

Sure, you can interpret this moving story very differently – it was just a coincidence that the light turned on like that and the father was imagining his beloved daughter holding his hands – but anyone who has lost a child or loved one will disagree. When the angels witness the anguish of a grieving parent they will try to find ways to reach out through meaningful signs that when recognized and understood by the recipient can bring huge comfort.

This next story is also about angels talking to us in ways that appear ordinary, but are anything but to the person involved during times of distress and darkness. For Andrea, listening to the prompting of her heart, and the voices in her dreams, gave her the strength to cope with her great loss.

Passed on

My grandfather passed away last year in February from cancer of the throat and stomach. I was very close to my grandfather. We talked loads on the phone. I shared all my problems with him and I saw him as much as possible even though I didn't live close by. Then about three years ago he was diagnosed with cancer. My family have a strong belief in an afterlife, but I wasn't sure about heaven until my grandfather started to visit a healer and got some of his strength back.

The doctors said it was a miracle, but whatever happened I was so grateful because I had another glorious six months with my grand-father and a chance for him to see me leave school and go on to a new job, which involved me travelling to New York. Before I left my grandfather gave me all the advice he could on what to do and what not to do, as he used to travel in his job a lot.

Sadly, when I was in New York my grandfather's cancer returned with a vengeance. I wasn't told about it while I was away, so I had no idea, but when I returned from New York my mum picked me up and took me straight to the hospital to see him. It was a great reunion and we talked and shared photos. He looked so ill but his face lit up when I came in. He also told me that while he had been in hospital he had seen a bright light come towards him, with a figure standing in the middle of the light. It stayed there for about two minutes and then disappeared.

My grandfather and I had never actually said the words 'I love you' to each other, but before I left the hospital that day I just felt this overwhelming urge to say it to him. I'm so glad I did tell him because no one thought he would deteriorate so quickly in the next few days. About four a.m. on the Thursday morning we got a phone call saying my mum needed to get to the hospital quickly because it wasn't looking good for my grandfather. When we woke up my stepdad told me Mum had gone down to help look after my grandfather. He died that afternoon.

I was distraught. I didn't get the chance to say goodbye to my grandfather. I cried for weeks on end. I missed him so much and the future looked dark without him. Then, three weeks after his death, I had a dream. The dream was so clear and felt so real. My mum, my aunt, my grandma and I were at my grandparents' old house. I was stood outside the living-room door. My family came out and told me, 'I'm sorry, Andrea, Grampie has just died.' I did not cry. I just walked into the room and saw my grandfather sitting with his eyes closed in his favourite blue chair. I sat down beside him and started to cry. He woke and said to me, 'Don't worry, Andrea, I'm fine. I love you so much and I will always be watching over you. Take care in your new job, when you are travelling, and remember I will always be at your side wherever you are. I love you,' and then he closed his eyes again and I woke up.

I have always believed and thought this really was my grandfather talking to me and letting me know everything is going to be fine, and giving me the opportunity to say goodbye. After my dream I felt a great warmth come over me, a sense of peace and love. I know that he hasn't left me, he is always there. He's just waiting for me in another place.

There's so much going on in Andrea's story – the presence of angels in Andrea herself when she listened to her heart and the presence of angels in her dreams. There's also the presence of angels in the healer who helped Andrea's grandfather regain a will to live, so she could share more precious time with him, not to mention her grandfather's angel vision.

Angels revealing a glimpse of themselves on earth through the words or actions of others during times of crisis and confusion is a theme that appears in Paul's story, below.

A door opens

A young teenager, aged seventeen, rang me to ask if I could help him because he was on the verge of suicide. As a counsellor I always respond quickly to people who are in this frame of minde. I visited him as soon as I could. He lived in a bedsit as he had left home and had had to take the only place that he could.

He opened the door to me and I was met by the sight of him dressed as a female, wearing a long wig. I introduced myself and then he asked me to refer to him as Lucy. He went on to tell me he had been disowned by his family because he grew up knowing that his feelings and emotions were those of a female and he was only happy when he was playing with girls and their dolls. He started to wear makeup in his early teens and when he reached sixteen, he told his family that he could not live as a male any more and said he wanted a sex change. He visited a doctor, who referred him to a specialist. The specialist told him that he could not have a full sex change until he was eighteen. He was adamant about the sex change and the specialist started to prepare him by giving him hormone therapy which prevented beard growth and enhanced his chest to form breasts.

I asked him why he was considering suicide now and he explained about his family disowning him and feeling confused and alone in the world. Then he said that he should have been born as a girl and not a boy. He said he was a female trapped inside a male body. He then informed me that there cannot be angels because if there were they would not have forced him to live a horrible life as a boy when he should have been a girl. He then told me about his plan to cut his wrists and how he knew exactly how to cut them so that he would not fail in his suicide.

I acted quickly and spoke from my heart. I told him that I believed angels and goodness did exist because he had been born into a country which was non-judgemental and liberal in its thinking, because this country embraces a tolerance of many things, including sex changes. I explained that he would probably not have had the choice to undergo a sex change if he had been born in a country with strict religious beliefs and laws. Therefore, angels do exist because they gave him the opportunity to become a female in a society that accepts people's rights to express themselves in whatever way they feel comfortable.

He smiled at me and told me that he felt a wave of relief sweep over him as he listened to me. He laughed and thanked me and promised me that he would not resort to suicide and would go ahead with the sex change.

He appeared on a documentary on television when he was eighteen and the operation had been successful.

Paul's story shows that we are all capable of being angels to one other. We can all let the angel inside us do the talking. We can all put aside our prejudices and become instruments of the extraordinary, lending to others simple words of encouragement, kindness and hope that can help them feel as if they have been touched by angels.

Why not me?

It seems clear to me from the extensive research I have done over the years that angels have the power to comfort people, physically, emotionally and spiritually, and to intervene during times of extreme stress or crisis to save lives. It is also clear that many of those who have been helped and healed by angels in whatever form they take during times of poor health, suffering or crisis have their faith and attitude to life transformed as a result. They can, perhaps for the first time in their lives, see light in the darkness.

All the stories so far in this book very clearly demonstrate this renewed sense of hope and purpose following angelic intervention, but I'm sure at some point there are those of you reading this with interest but still in your mind you are asking yourselves the question so many people have asked me since I began writing angel books. Why do the angels sometimes intervene during times of suffering, and sometimes not? Why do they answer one person's prayers and not another's?

The news keeps us up-to-date with every natural disaster and the newspapers keep us informed of personal tragedies, injustices and unimaginable sufferings. Where were the angels when an earthquake struck the people of Haiti in early 2010? Where were the angels when terrorist attacks rocked the world? Where was Baby P's angel? Where are the angels when a boy of five suffers horribly and dies from cancer? I could go on and on.

How I wish I could give you an answer to this question, a question that every seeker of spiritual truth asks themselves at some point in their lives, but it is a question that is impossible for me or anyone to answer while we live on earth. It seems our angels know things about the world of spirit that we cannot, and it is beyond our understanding why they manifest on one occasion and not another. Perhaps it is only when we have crossed over to the other side that we will begin to see the bigger picture of our lives and everyone else's lives. All I know is that there is a reason for everything, even suffering and loss, and it seems that it is often pain and tragedy which moves us to go within to seek answers and try to make sense of it all.

And it seems that the best sense we get is the truth we discover for ourselves, when the angel within speaks to us and we just 'know' all the answers. Not how to avoid suffering and challenges, but how to cope with them and how to know that whatever happens to us, somehow, somewhere we are protected and loved beyond measure. This was certainly the case for Fiona, who suffered intolerable abuse as a child.

Bath time

Childhood is supposed to be the happiest time of your life — that's what people often say, isn't it? But for me it was a blur of pain, fear and confusion. I was seven when my mum became an alcoholic. I've been told she wasn't a heavy drinker when I was born, but I have no memories of her without the smell of alcohol on her breath. My dad walked out when I was a toddler and I've never had any contact with him since — I'm unlikely to either as the word is that he has moved to

Australia with a girl half his age. He's got a brand-new family now. I think, like me, he just wants to leave the past behind.

Again, I can't remember when Mum started to hit me and lock me in my room for long hours, while she drank herself to an early grave, because it always seemed to be that way. In some weird, confusing ways I preferred the beatings because at least she was aware of me. I was getting attention from her. The worst part was being locked in my room while she slept off her hangover. It was not unusual at the weekends for me to be locked in late Friday night and let out on Sunday evening. I became an expert at reading her moods, and once tried to run away when I could sense that she was getting violent again, but well-meaning neighbours found me and brought me back. When they came round Mum was all smiles and concern. She was good, you see, at pretending everything was OK and hiding her addiction. She'd wash her mouth out with peppermint and use air freshener round the house. However drunk she was she'd always make sure I got to school on time with the right uniform. If she hit me it would always be on my back or high up on my arms where no one could see. I was so young nobody believed me when I said Mum drank a lot. It was the 1960s, and 'grown-ups' would just smile at me in a patronizing way and say, 'Everybody likes a drink.'

I guess with no one to reach out to I just retreated into my shell. Running away wasn't an option as there was nowhere for me to go. This was my life. I was getting what I deserved. I was an ugly, badly behaved child.

Then one day when I was about nine, Mum came home and she was scarier than ever. By this I mean she was being nice to me, very nice. It always started that way. She apologized over and over and then I would do something or say something and for reasons I could not understand she would fly off the handle. She told me she was going to run me a nice bath. She'd got me some bath essence and was going to pour it in. As I watched her run the bath the fear – or perhaps the sight of the running water – got to me and I wet my underwear.

I tried to hide it but Mum was eagle-eyed and spotted the tell-tale signs on the bathroom floor. What happened then is forever burned into my memory and my heart. Everything went into slow motion. I saw Mum shouting and screaming but I didn't hear her. I saw her raise her fists at me but I didn't feel anything. I looked at the running bath water and, rising up from the bubbles, I saw this shining figure emerge. Huge wings came out from behind it and it wrapped its arms around me. For the first time in my life I felt loved and not alone.

In an instant the figure was gone and I found myself standing there next to Mum with bubbles all around my body. I looked at her and everything felt different. She looked frightened of me. She backed away and locked herself in her bedroom.

After that day until I left home at the age of seventeen, I'm not saying that Mum never hit me or shouted at me again. She did, but it was never as severe as before. Perhaps it had something to do with the fact that around that time I had a growth spurt and was taller than before and not as easy to bully, but I think it is down to much more than that. I think my mum saw the strength of my guardian angel rising up in me.

I've never been able to ask Mum what happened that day because ten months after I had left she died. It wasn't the drink that killed her in the end, it was her heart – she had a stroke. I didn't go to her funeral – I don't think many did – and I don't even know where her ashes were scattered. One day I might try to find out but right now I'm busy being a mum myself to four gorgeous kids of my own. The other day my youngest daughter, Ellie, brought me a beautiful card for Mother's Day. She wrote a poem about me in it saying lovely things, and the other three clubbed together to buy me a coat I've had my eye on. Whenever I read Ellie's card and wear that coat, the feeling I get inside me is so much like the feeling I got when my guardian angel hugged me at bath time.

Fiona sent me her story because she wanted it to be read by others who may also have gone through periods of terrible darkness in their lives. She hoped it would be of comfort because it shows that within each one of us there is always a source of courage, strength, dignity and light that injustice, tragedy, hate, cruelty and misfortune cannot extinguish. She wanted others to know that there is love in the world, light in the darkness, and however dark and difficult your journey gets love is always stronger than hate.

Like Fiona, Grace also hopes that her story will help others see glimmers of light during periods of intolerable darkness.

Remember?

After my dad was diagnosed with the early stages of Alzheimer's there were days when he was completely normal but there were also days when he would leave his house and just wander for miles with no idea where he was going. I was concerned for his safety and so he moved in with me and my husband, Ben. This arrangement just about worked for eighteen months but then Dad started to behave really erratically. Night-times were the worst. He would drift around the house rearranging the furniture. He also became incontinent and started to shout at the children and call them names.

I staggered on for the next two years as best I could but by the time my dad was sixty-five I was getting desperate. My biggest concern was for the safety of my children, especially now that Dad was lighting matches for no reason. I asked for help from my doctor but the more I asked for help the more tests my dad was sent for and the more forms I had to fill in. I felt trapped.

My dad found it hard to even remember my name. He'd look at me as if I was a stranger or an enemy. One night when I was trying to get him to rest he started shouting and accusing me of kidnapping him. It took four hours to settle him and I fell into bed in the small hours of the morning, totally burned out. I was so tired that I couldn't sleep and I just lay there crying. Ever since I left school I'd been too busy working and earning money and raising a family. I had stopped thinking about or believing in any higher power but that night I begged for someone to help me and to help my dad. I knew this was bigger than me and I asked my guardian angel to guide me.

All of a sudden I saw a ball of light flicker beside my bed. I rubbed my eyes to make sure I wasn't seeing things and crawled to the bottom of my bed to take a closer look. Then I saw an angel. It was fairly small, about the size of a football, and it was just floating at the bottom of the bed. It had bright golden wings and a long gown that sparkled with light. It was the most beautiful thing I have ever seen and as I gazed in wonder the most amazing feeling of peace came over me.

The angel floated towards me and I felt all the tension leave my body. I felt warmth come over my body. The angel hovered in front of me for a few minutes and then it vanished. I knew then that everything was going to work out fine.

My husband was asleep the whole time. I know it wasn't a hallucination because from that night onwards it felt as if a weight had lifted off my shoulders. The next morning social services called and I was told that a home help would be visiting for a couple of hours every day to give me a break. It meant I could start to get my life back together again.

For the next three years Dad's condition got steadily worse and in the last six months of his life he didn't recognize me at all. Despite this I still felt that there was a strong connection between us and sometimes he would look at me as if he knew what I was thinking. I also felt his love for me. The day before he died he woke up and raised his arms towards me. When I came over he looked at me and said my name. I longed for him to say more but my name was enough. My dad had remembered me, at last. The next day he slipped into unconsciousness and passed away gently in his sleep.

Although my dad's illness weighed heavily on his family my guardian angel gave me the strength I needed to cope when I was at my lowest. She opened my eyes to the world of spirit and this made losing Dad so much easier to bear.

Grace's awesome story is uncommon because she actually saw an angel, and as mentioned previously angels prefer to reveal themselves in more subtle ways, but I have included it here not just because it is a stunning example of an angel encounter changing a person's life for the better, but because I think it illustrates brilliantly something I have often noticed when reading and compiling angel stories. And this is that on a number of occasions simply thinking about the possibility of angels guiding your life can change your feelings from uncertainty, loneliness and fear to feelings of peace, comfort and certainty. And it is this change from fear and loneliness to hope and expectation, rather than the angel encounter itself, that is the real miracle. In other words, inner peace, and the renewed sense of hope, purpose and possibility this brings, is the catalyst for divine intervention and positive life change.

Alison, who is gradually coming to terms with the loss of the man she loved dearly, describes this feeling of inner peace far better than I have:

So much better now

I've had many experiences of Mike coming to visit me. He is not always with me; he goes off on his trips, probably walking the mountains that he loved to visit. Being a military man he would often go off on these jaunts and get back to nature so I do not worry that he has gone away and won't be back. I feel so much better now, more confident and less alone, but don't get me wrong, I miss him terribly and wish that things could have been different — but they aren't so I just have to get on with it and make the most of my life. Positive thinking keeps me strong. Do you know what I mean when I say I have an inner peace, a tranquil feeling that is hard to describe to people who do not have it? I think you will know what I mean; it is a bizarre but beautiful feeling of elation.

This 'bizarre but beautiful feeling of elation' following periods of despair or hopelessness is something I have experienced on many occasions in my life. But just because I have had these wonderful breakthroughs in awareness, doesn't mean that I have lost my fears and doubts completely. I have often found myself questioning my angels again, but what has changed is that this questioning doesn't unsettle me nearly as much as it used to, because deep down I know it will pass. I have finally understood that experiencing fear and doubt comes with being human. It is part of the experience of living, the journey of our lives, which is the theme of the next chapter.

Returning to this chapter, even those who have had the most dramatic angel encounters, seen lights in the darkness, never lose their insecurities completely. The intensity of the experience tends to fade as the harsh realities of everyday life settle back in. But in some ways this return to reality is a good thing. We need to experience weakness and doubt, because without that weakness we would never be able to recognize strength and courage within ourselves. We would never be able to experience the awesome power of faith, and faith by definition is belief in something without proof or evidence, or when there is reason to doubt.

Angel encounters will always give us reason to doubt, because in the great majority of cases the proof angels offer us for their existence is so personal and elusive. Remember, it is not the fact that we have doubts about our angels that matters – it is how we respond to those doubts. We can respond with cynicism, distrust and fear to the possibility of miracles or we can respond with courage, hope and heart. And it doesn't take much to work out which path in life will lead us to greater happiness.

Rest assured, your guardian angel is always at your side urging you to listen to your heart. This is why, regardless of whether or not you think you have had an angel encounter yourself, simply reading stories of hope when all hope is lost, like the ones in this book, can be acts of healing and transformation themselves by helping to draw the awesome power of faith in the miraculous back into your life. Some of the stories you may not relate to, others may intrigue you, others may astonish you, but I'm hoping there will always be at least one that lingers in your thoughts, like the lyrics to a song or tune you can't get out of your mind. Keep your thoughts focused on that story, read it over and over again, because it could be the channel your angels have chosen to call out to you, urging you to refresh your faith in the everlasting power of goodness, love and hope in this world and the next.

Believing in angels won't make everything in your life perfect, end all suffering, take away all your worries and concerns or solve all your problems. What it will do, though, is help you see that there is always a part of you, an eternal part, that can transcend, or rise above, anything life throws at you, however painful or difficult it may feel. And when you reconnect with that eternal part of yourself, when feelings of love, goodness and hope re-emerge in your heart, there is only ever a bright light to follow and a never-ending song in your heart.

CHAPTER 5

The Journey of Life

Beside each person who's born on earth
A guardian angel takes its stand to guide him
through life's mysteries.

Menander of Athens

Angels: does it matter what form they take, if we believe that we have encountered one? As a feeling, an insight, in a dream, seeing them shimmering in the darkness, glowing in radiant white robes with a vitality not of this world or in the guise of cloud, a song, a picture, a hug, a meaningful coincidence or the actions of a kind stranger. However they appear, does it really matter as long as angel encounters bring with them an awareness of the life-transforming truth that whatever our age, background and circumstances in this life we are never alone?

An angel walks beside us and loves us in every age and stage of our lives and in this chapter, fittingly the longest chapter in the book because it will take you on a journey from cradle to beyond the grave, you'll see that miracles can happen at any stage in a person's life, from conception – and sometimes even before that – through baby- and childhood, into teenage and adult life towards old age and the very end, and for ever after that.

Let's start at the very beginning with some stories about angel encounters during pregnancy and birth. The creation of new life is a miracle, so it does not surprise me that a high number of the angel stories that have been sent to me over the years are associated with conception, pregnancy and birth. I'd like to get things started with Janet's intriguing story.

A knock on the door

I'd been trying for five years to get pregnant and my fortieth birthday was fast approaching. I'd tried everything conventional and alternative medicine could offer – had two rounds of IVF – and still no success. All I had ever wanted was to be a mother. Even as a little girl I used to rock my little sister and sing her to sleep. I was the most sought-after babysitter with my friends but now I wanted to have a baby myself. Trouble was, we were running out of money and I had just started what we had agreed would be our last course of treatment. To say I felt anxious was an understatement.

Anyway, it was the night before I would find out the results and I just couldn't settle at all. I longed for good news but in my mind I was convinced that I was never going to be a mother and for the first time I'd seriously discussed the possibility of adoption with Simon, my partner. That hadn't really given me the comfort I thought it would because even though he didn't say it I could tell that he was only doing it to make me happy – if he had a choice he would prefer not to adopt because what he really wanted was his own child. Perhaps he would tire of it all and find another woman who could give him a child? Perhaps I would have to go through the adoption process alone? I don't think I have ever felt so low. I just sat in the kitchen for hours with my head in my hands, wondering why my life had all gone wrong.

It must have been about nine p.m. when I heard a knock on my door. Wiping away my tears I went to find out who it was and could not believe my eyes when I saw that it was my grandma. She couldn't have chosen a better time to come and see me. Last time I had seen her she was feeling quite poorly and confined to her bed. That must have been about two months ago. Well, she looked healthy and happy now and I immediately let her in and put the kettle on. Nights were always tough for me when Simon was on his shift and it was so like Grandma to know that I needed the company on this of all nights when I was awaiting my results.

We talked for a good hour or so and I told her all my worries and fears about the possibility of adoption. She didn't say much but the fact that she was just listening to me gave me such a feeling of comfort and peace. Then she said I was not to worry because I would conceive and I would have a baby daughter. I asked her how she could be so sure and she just laughed and said it was 'grandma' wisdom. She smiled so mischievously that I couldn't help but laugh too and, not having laughed for a while, it felt really good. Instinctively, I reached out to her and for a few glorious seconds we hugged but then when I drew away and opened my eyes she had gone. She had vanished into thin air. How could that be?

111

I called out to her down the street but there was no sign of her. Had I imagined it all? Was this the first sign of madness? Had I fallen asleep and dreamed it all? I called my mum to tell her that Grandma had visited but Mum told me what I was saying was impossible because Grandma was at home with Granddad. I called Granddad and he confirmed that Grandma had been at home all the time, in a very deep and peaceful sleep. My grandparents live over fifteen miles away so to this day I don't know how Grandma visited me. I could tell that everyone thought I was imagining things so I soon shut up about it and went to bed.

The next morning the phone rang and I was told that sadly I wasn't pregnant. I surprised myself and Simon with the calm way I received the news, but then this had been the news I was expecting. It was time now to leave the fertility treatments behind and look at other alternatives – perhaps adoption, perhaps fostering; I didn't know, but what I did know was that it was the end of something and the beginning of something new. I even felt a glimmer of hope growing inside me and it was mixed with relief that I would not have to go through the emotional rollercoaster of fertility treatment again.

So, there I was taking the bad news much better than expected when about half an hour later there was a knock on the door. Simon went to get it this time and I nearly fell over backwards with shock when my fertility specialist walked into my living room. He told me that as soon as he heard he had to come and deliver the news personally. Somehow there had been a mix-up with the test results and I'd been given the wrong results. I was pregnant.

Seven months later my beautiful little girl – Sandra – was born. She was several weeks premature but she was a real fighter and is now a healthy and very talkative four-year-old. Just writing down this story for you has made me relive it all over again and I find it hard to believe myself, so can totally understand why others may struggle to believe it too. One day, though, when she is old enough I am going to tell Sandra about it. I did tell my grandma when she recovered from her illness but she clearly didn't understand what I was talking about. She was just happy to see me happy and to become a great-grandmother. Do you think my guardian angel used the image of my grandmother to comfort me or was it all in my imagination? Was I hallucinating? I know I was feeling stressed and anxious but the experience felt so real and so reassuring.

I wrote back to tell Janet that this was one of the most intriguing stories I have read – and believe me I have read many astonishing stories in my time. I also told her that in my mind there is no doubt that the experience was real for her and that somehow her guardian angel – or perhaps even the out-of-body spirit of her grandmother or even little Sandra – visited her to offer her comfort and hope when she needed it the most.

Janet's story is similar in some ways to other stories I've been sent by mothers who tell me that they conceived or found out they were pregnant following the visit of a guardian angel. Becky's story is a good example.

Touched by an angel

We'd been trying for a baby for almost a year. I wasn't yet at the stage when I felt the need to visit a doctor but getting pregnant was rising on my list of priorities. I did want to become a mother. Then one night I fell asleep and woke up in the middle of the night with this incredible feeling of warmth and strength flowing through me. It energized me so much that I sat up and thought about getting up to do some reading or housework. When I sat up I saw a glowing white light – well it was more cream-coloured – flowing towards me. It didn't frighten me at all, quite the opposite. I wanted it to come towards me and when it surrounded me it felt like I was stepping into a warm bath. It was so relaxing I lay back down and settled back to sleep. Two weeks later I did a pregnancy test and it was positive. I am convinced that the night I felt the touch of an angel was the night I conceived.

I'm not surprised in any way that angels may reveal themselves at the moment of conception – when the miracle of new life is created – just as I'm not surprised that they also seem to appear during pregnancy, when the miracle of new life is being nurtured. Gloria, whose story is below, once dismissed the idea of angels as ridiculous, but she changed her mind when she was fourteen weeks pregnant with her first child.

Be patient and trust

I had a really vivid dream when I was about thirteen or fourteen weeks pregnant with my first child. In this dream there was a man I recognized from photographs in our family album as the doctor who had delivered me. He died about thirty years ago in a car accident but in my dream he was alive and real. He told me that he couldn't deliver my baby for me. I started to cry and say I wanted to keep her but he said she would be well looked after. He put a hand on my shoulder and told me to be patient and to trust because things would be bright again after a period of darkness. After he had spoken to me I felt happy and soothed.

When I woke up I had an instinctive feeling that something was not right with my baby. My fears were confirmed the next day when a sonogram couldn't detect a heartbeat. There wasn't much support from the hospital, beyond 'you can always try again, and my only real source of comfort was the dream I had had. I knew that my baby was somewhere and being cared for.

Just as my dream predicted there was a period of darkness following my miscarriage. I got very down and spent a lot of time sulking and finding it hard to even be in the same room or space as another pregnant woman. I did often think of my dream but sometimes it made me feel worse because I wanted to be comforted again by something similar, and I wasn't.

I wasn't trying for a baby, because I still hadn't got over the loss of my first, but ten months later I found out I was pregnant. You can imagine just how anxious I was second time around. I stayed in bed for ten days when I approached the fourteen-week landmark. Doctors told me that this wouldn't make any difference as to whether or not I miscarried but I wasn't going to take any risks.

When the fourteen weeks came and went I did start to worry a little less, but it was still a scary time. But then I started to find these white feathers wherever I went. I did some research and read one of your books and found out that white feathers are often a sign of angels walking by your side. My first baby was a girl and I would have called

115

her Heather. I'm wondering if there is any significance in that feather is so similar-sounding to Heather. Perhaps she is watching over me during my pregnancy. Perhaps she is my guardian-angel baby.

I'm thirty-seven weeks now and my baby boy is due to be born very soon. It would be wonderfully comforting to know that in spirit my Heather is watching over us both.

I kept in touch with Gloria and found out that she gave birth to a healthy little boy, called Harry. She continues to tell me that she believes her angel baby is never far away. Sixteen-year-old Sam, whose story is below, also believes her guardian-angel baby hasn't left her.

She lives in me

In August 1992, eleven months before I was born, my only sister died at three days old. Ever since I was little I have wanted to know more about her and have always hoped she is watching over me. In the past few years I have thought about her a lot more and sometimes I swear I can feel her brush my hair out of my face when I'm upset and kiss my forehead.

I have been having a tough time the past few years so maybe that is why I am thinking of her more. My mum is an alcoholic and I no longer see her because of that and there has been a lot of exam stress which has really got my mood down. It seems when times get tough my sister will always be there telling me to carry on and stay strong. Telling me she will always love me. I have never seen her like I'd love to but sometimes I feel her presence. Sometimes the one thing that keeps me going is the fact that I should live for her and should live life to the full because she never got to live at all.

When I wrote back to Sam I told her that as long as the presence she senses is comforting and supportive then she can have no doubt it is her sister reaching out to her in spirit. And not only is her sister all around her she is also living inside her, within her heart. Sam should never lose sight of that as she leaves child-hood behind and begins her journey into adulthood.

To return to the theme of pregnancy and birth, here's another interesting story sent to me by Lynn.

Due date

It was close to a week after my due date and I was getting rather anxious and fretful and uncomfortable. I'd delivered my first and second child well before my due dates and had expected I'd do the same for my third. Eventually, I had to be induced and it was a pretty distressing experience because my baby's head was very large and I needed to be cut. I've always favoured natural births but this time it was so painful I begged for drugs, only to be told that the only option left to me at this advanced stage of labour was gas and air.

For hours the labour dragged on. It felt as if my child really didn't want to come out, didn't want to be born. I was exhausted and went to another place at one point. It felt as if I was going down a tunnel. I was heading towards a golden light. I felt as if something was hold-ing me, rocking me like a baby and a feeling of incredible peace was everywhere. Then I saw the shape of golden wings and I realized it was an angel, telling me my baby just wanted a little more time and everything would be OK. It was so reassuring.

The next thing I know I've woken up in another room and my husband is sitting beside me. My new baby is in a trolley beside my bed. My husband told me I'd given everyone a bit of a scare because I lost a lot of blood and fainted, but I'd pulled through and the baby was fine.

There's a beautiful story in the Talmud that tells how before a baby is born it is cared for and loved by the angels, but when the time comes for it to be born an angel kisses it just above the lips and below the nose – the groove called the philtrum – to make it forget all that it has learned, otherwise it would long to return to the world of spirit. Perhaps Lynn's baby wasn't quite ready to leave all that love and wisdom behind and just needed to linger a while longer with the angels before making his grand entrance into the world.

If you thought these stories were astonishing, see what you think about this one, sent in by Jo.

The little girl of my dreams

I wasn't trying for a baby. I wasn't really in a serious relationship. Babies were the very last thing on my mind. I was just casually dating and I'm not ashamed to say, having fun doing it. One night after chatting to my best friend – she had just found out she was pregnant – I had a dream that seemed to last all night.

In my dream I was taking to a little girl. She had red hair and blue/green eyes and we just chatted about everyone and everything. Even though she was very young I felt so comfortable and carefree with her. I really liked her and when I woke up in the morning I missed her. I missed the feeling of closeness and connection between us.

In the months that followed I would meet this little girl in my dreams every few weeks. It was always such a happy experience. We'd just spend hours talking and laughing and playing. I don't know what we talked about but it was brilliant. I felt so close to her but I didn't even know her name.

Then a year after my dreams started I found out I was pregnant. As soon as the pregnancy test turned positive I just knew I was going to keep my baby, even though I wasn't sure who the father was. This sounds daft but I looked forward to meeting the little girl in my dreams and telling her my good news but the dreams just stopped. Then when my baby daughter was born with a hint of golden red hair and bright blue eyes, I again just knew she was the girl of my dreams.

My daughter is fifteen years old now and the light of my life – she changed my life for the better in every possible way. I'm even a married and respectable woman now. I have also been blessed with two sons, but my connection with my daughter is as strong as ever. Just as we did in my dreams we spend hours talking, laughing and having fun together. She means the world to me. She's the daughter of my dreams.

Jo did talk to her friends and family about her dreams but no one believed her and so she stopped talking about it, until she read one of my books and sent this story to me. I encouraged her to tell her daughter as I was convinced that her daughter would believe her. I was right.

Olga also believes her child 'knew' her or 'chose' her to be his mother. Here's her story:

An angel chose me

I am very interested in angels and I know I have had an angel experience myself, which I would like to share it with you. It was back in December 1974. I already had a daughter who was almost four and I had been trying for another baby for about two years. I was very happy having a daughter because I only wanted to have baby girls; I didn't feel I could handle a boy — not so much as a baby but as an adult. I was convinced that I only wanted another baby girl. So much so that I told all my friends and family that I never wanted a boy and constantly repeated this to them.

It was a cold December morning and just before I woke up, I heard a voice. Neither a man nor woman's voice which I now know is a sign that it is an angel voice. This voice said very clearly, 'If you say you will have a boy, you can have one straightaway.' I immediately woke up and told my husband about this voice and he asked me what my answer was to this question. I replied, 'I didn't answer' and he said, 'Don't you think you should have? You should have said yes.'

I thought about this long and hard and decided it MUST be some kind of test because heaven wouldn't have been cruel enough to give me a boy! Also I told my best friend the next day, who was a nurse, and she thought it was weird. In my own mind I just said, 'OK then, I'll have a boy.' Then I discovered I was pregnant! Still not thinking I would have a boy all through the pregnancy, I gave birth to my darling son on 2 October 1975. Everyone felt sorry for me and thought I would be devastated because the child was a boy but I bonded with him immediately and we have a very, very close relationship now and always have had. Since reading more about angels I can see this experience is quite 'normal' and a baby does choose its parents, before it is born.

The idea of connecting with a future child before they are born may seem unbelievable. It's easier perhaps to accept the dreams and intuitions and 'knowing' feelings that come later, during pregnancy, but what a joy to think that in our dreams we may be able to meet our child before they are even conceived.

'Meeting' your future child before they are actually born is in fact more common than you might think. I myself remember having vivid dreams of my son when I was pregnant with him. They faded from memory until he reached the age of four or five, when it became clear to me that the child I had encountered in my dream was my own son. In my dream I was trying to climb up a mountain but failing miserably. A little boy appeared and offered me a hand and with his help I reached the top. That boy was the spitting image of my son, with the same big brown eyes, dark brown hair and most noticeably with a cowlick on the lefthand side of his forehead, just like my son has today. And just as he does today, in my dream he was encouraging me to push myself and go further than I thought I could. He helped me climb a mountain in my dreams, and today he is the first to criticize me whenever I become defeatist in any way about my work and my ability to do it. He believes in me and in achieving the impossible and I'm learning from his positivity every day.

Some pre-conception stories bring news of the pregnancy to an unsuspecting mother- or father-to-be. This was certainly the case for Monica, who had no idea she was pregnant until an angel called her name.

An angel spoke to me

I was chatting with my mum – can't even remember what it was about, but it wasn't about getting pregnant or babies. Suddenly I heard a voice. It was inside my head but outside of it as well and it seemed to come from just above my right ear. It's never happened to me before or since but it told me that the reason I had been feeling tired lately was because I had invited someone into my life and that someone was with me now. He was here. My mum didn't really notice that I had switched off while she was talking to me, as she was knitting and speaking at the same time. I felt so light and warm, as if I had been hugged by my mum. Two days later I found out I was pregnant.

I could go on and on here with stories that have been sent to me by parents – both mums and dads – who have glimpsed their child's face in a dream or felt a loving presence, or just had a sudden flash of knowing something about their future child. These stories are awesome and wonderful and if you're reading this and hoping one day to be a parent, keep your inner eyes and ears open! Someone may be trying to get in touch . . .

I'd like to press forward now on our journey from stories about pregnancy and birth to stories about babies and young children. Chances are, you may already have heard or read miraculous rescue stories involving young children and babies where the presence of an angel seems perhaps to be the only possible explanation. Stories like these astonishing ones which caught my eye in the newspapers and on the internet in the last few years.

Miracle escape for baby in pram

This incredible story hit the press in October 2009, and attracted the interest of US talkshow queen Oprah Winfrey. It involved a six-month-old baby who had a miraculous escape when his pram was struck by a suburban train in Melbourne, Australia. The baby's pram rolled off a platform at Ashburton railway station about four p.m. and into the path of an oncoming train that pushed it some thirty metres along the track. Fortunately, the baby was eventually pulled to safety by a young man and the only injury sustained was a bump on the head.

Disposable nappy saves a baby's life

This story, which hit the headlines in August 2008, would not seem out of place in a cartoon, but it is all true. According to media reports a disposable nappy saved the life of an eighteen-month-old boy, breaking his fall from a third-floor apartment window. Baby Caua Felipe Massaneiro survived a thirty-foot (ten-metre) fall because his nappy snagged on a security spike embedded in the concrete wall around his apartment building in the northeastern Brazilian city of Recife. The boy dangled from the spike for a moment, then the nappy opened and the baby fell to the ground, but at a much slower speed. The nappy obviously lessened the impact of the fall and saved the baby's life. 'It was a miracle,' said the officer, who declined to be identified because she was not authorized to speak to the press. 'He could also have been killed by one of the spikes.'

I read this next captivating story reported in UK newspapers in January 2010. It's about a four-month-old boy called Alfie who earned the nickname 'the living miracle' after a hospital administration error saved him from dying in the womb.

The living miracle

According to media reports Alfie could have died several months before he was due to be born, after complications with the placenta. His parents had no idea there was any problem with their firstborn child because they had been told at a twenty-week scan that he was perfectly healthy and normal.

Fortunately, the problem was spotted when Aflie's mother was called in for another scan six weeks later – by mistake. Alfie was delivered by emergency Caesarean section weighing just 1lb 5oz, but within months he steadily gained weight and was able to go back home with his parents. There is no doubt that if he hadn't been called in by mistake for this non-routine scan at the Princess Anne Neonatal Unit in Southampton, Alfie could well have died and his parents would have discovered there was a problem only when movement stopped in the womb.

Alfie's mother did at one point consider telling the hospital that another scan was an administrative error, but she couldn't resist the opportunity to see her baby on a scan again so she and her husband went back to the hospital. She is quoted in the *Daily Mail* as saying that fate changed everything. Things could have been very different and she may have had to walk out of hospital without her son. She believes somebody was definitely watching over her family.

That 'something' was, I believe, an angel. All these stories got a lot of attention from the press but as is often the case with 'miracle' stories of this kind, I've been sent stories that are similar in every way, except for the fact that they weren't publicized for one reason or another. I've been sent mystifying stories of children surviving car crashes and accidents and other dangerous situations against all odds and in each case parents or carers are convinced, as Alfie's mum was in the previous story, that something unseen was watching over and protecting their child. Stories like this one sent to me by Nicola.

What if . . .

I'd love your thoughts on this story. At the time I put it down to my intuition but after reading some of your books I think it may have been something more. It happened three years ago, when my son was six or seven months old. I woke up in the middle of the night – it was just after one a.m. as I checked the clock – and the house was very quiet. I don't know why I woke up or why I jumped out of bed and went into the hall outside my bedroom. I thank heaven every day that

I did because I found my son crawling close to the staircase. He was so close he could easily have fallen down the stairs. I grabbed him before he toppled over and the next morning bought some higher bars to put on his cot so he could not get out again. Something saved my baby from injury or worse that night. Every time I think of it, including right now as I'm writing to you, I get goosebumps. What if . . .

I wrote back to tell Nicola that the voice of our intuition is so often the voice of our inner angel speaking to us. Every moment of our lives there are voices running through our heads. Many of those voices are the voices of fear and self-doubt, and I'm often asked by my readers how they can tell if their guardian angel is speaking to them. My reply is always the same: the voice of your guardian angel will always be clear, gentle and encouraging, whereas the voice of your ego will be confusing, conflicting and negative. In short, when your guardian angel speaks to you, you will just know what to do; there will not be any long-drawn-out explanations, or any feelings of fear and doubt, just a calm and quiet knowing.

Betsy followed the voice of her inner angel and is eternally grateful that she did. Here's her story:

Sleeping through

When Olivia was born, my husband and I had done a lot of reading and we both agreed that she should settle into a good night-time routine in her own bed as soon as possible. Trouble is, Olivia had ideas of her own. Night-times became pure torture. She would scream and scream for hours, settling only when she was picked up. We were exhausted. The most she ever slept in her cot was three hours. It was driving us mad. I talked to my doctor, who sent a midwife round to advise us. She basically told us that we were being too soft and that we had to be firm. We should not pick her up every time she cried. I was sceptical at first but her techniques worked. The first week was horrible. I didn't think I could go through with it — I wanted to rush in and comfort my baby — but I persisted and within three weeks Olivia had learned that screaming during the night wasn't going to get Mummy and Daddy rushing in.

It was bliss getting a good night's sleep after all that time, but then one night as I was getting ready for bed with Olivia sleeping peacefully in her room, I had this irrational urge to hold her. I tried to fight it because this would upset all the order we had created around bedtime, but it just got stronger and stronger. I just couldn't sleep so I tiptoed out of bed and went into her room. I could hear her gently snoring and gazed down at her. Without thinking I reached out and picked her up and cuddled her. It was the best feeling in the world. She didn't even wake up. After a few minutes I thought about putting her back in her cot but I just couldn't. I needed her close to me so I tiptoed back to bed and went to sleep with her in my arms.

When I woke up my husband wasn't nearly as cross as I thought he might be, but I knew that I was setting myself up for trouble by sending Olivia mixed signals. I thought I'd been very selfish but everything changed in my mind when I went to her nursery and saw that the ceiling above her cot had collapsed. I'll never know for sure but I'm pretty certain if Olivia had been in there she would not have survived.

Intuition isn't a theme in John's story, but it's clear from his incredible account that something was following and watching over his son.

In the arms of an angel

I was walking across a road and carrying my son in his car seat. A car appeared out of nowhere and hit me. I was thrown onto the ground and my son's car seat flew out of my hands. The miracle is that neither I nor my son were seriously hurt. We had cuts and bruises but nothing was broken. I can remember this huge bang and then falling down. I didn't feel any pain. All I thought about was my son. Many people have told me that it was a blessing that he was securely strapped into his car seat, but I believe that angels caught him when I fell and gently placed him down.

'It must be a miracle' life-saving angel stories like this may force even the most cynical of people to at the very least consider the possibility that an unseen presence is close by watching over a baby or child, but as mind-blowing as such stories are, it is important to get a sense of perspective and to remind ourselves once again that they are rare. Far more common are stories where the child involved is not in a life-or-death situation, and yet there is a strong sense that guardian angels are close by. These stories may not be as sensational, but to those involved they are every bit as miraculous. Here's a lovely story sent to me by Anne Marie about her daughter Cressy.

Sent from above

This happened just recently when Cressy had the baby. She had a painful labour with a difficult, even more painful ventouse delivery. Immediately after the baby was born, the midwives said he had a temperature, but within minutes they said he was too cold. He was taken to the special-care baby unit to be looked after and warmed up, separating him from Cressy, who of course was in floods of tears. Cressy and the baby stayed in hospital for a few days — longer than is normal nowadays. Although Cressy strongly wanted to breastfeed, the staff seemed more interested in getting calories into the baby in whatever way to help him stay warm than they were in helping her establish breastfeeding.

Soon after birth they put a feeding tube through his nose down to his stomach, but because Cressy hated that, eventually she agreed to them giving him a top-up bottle. When I went to visit, Cressy was tearful and finding it difficult to get the baby latched on at the breast, and I felt unless something was done soon, he would end up being totally bottle-fed — against both his mother's and father's wishes (and mine!). When I went home I deliberately prayed for a 'breast-feeding angel'. In my mind, I imagined an angel coming and, though invisible, somehow helping Cressy to get the knowledge and strength to breastfeed.

That night one of my friends rang me to ask how Cressy was getting on. She told me that her daughter, Olivia, a trainee midwife — nineteen years old — was going to be on Cressy's ward the next day; although she is training in Portsmouth, she was doing hours at the hospital local to her home over the Christmas holidays. When I went in to see Cressy, she said that Olivia had been in to see her and it was nice to see someone that she had last seen quite a few years ago. Olivia also popped in when I was there and I told her my concerns about the breastfeeding. She said she would come back and try to help Cressy later.

That evening Cressy rang me to say that Olivia had stayed with her for forty minutes, suggested different breastfeeding positions, helped and calmed her, and also explained to the other professionals on the ward that Cressy wanted to breastfeed exclusively. I was so relieved, and it was only much later on that I realized that Olivia was the breastfeeding angel that I had asked for! A totally human girl ... but there, in the right place at the right time. Truly sent to help, I totally believe! And from then to now, Cressy has had no real problems with breastfeeding.

Just as angels can speak to us through our intuition, they can also express their love and support through the angel inside of other people. Sara, whose story follows below, also believes that angels surround her baby.

Undulating blue lights

When I had my first baby two years ago, a daughter, I started having strange experiences during the night when I was feeding her and changing her nappy. No lights would be on in the house as I changed her nappy in the small hours of morning, and no lights were on in the street. I could see enough to do what I had to do. As I changed her, I began seeing what I can only describe as a blue glow around her tummy. This behaved differently to sparks, because it lasted a lot longer, three or four seconds of undulating blue light. I would shake my head, blink my eyes, and move my hands away to make sure that what I was seeing was not some kind of mind/eye trick. But the dancing light remained.

I stopped seeing these lights around my baby because I stopped changing her during the night once she started to sleep through. But I began seeing the lights again when I had my son six months ago. Again, these lights appeared when I was changing/feeding in the middle of the night. The only difference was that his light is white. I don't know if these are angels that I see. But I definitely didn't feel alone when they appeared.

Like Sara, countless parents and grandparents have got in touch with me in the years I've been an angel author to tell me that they are convinced their babies or grandchildren have guardian angels watching over them. An equal number have also written to me to tell me that they think babies and children have the ability to see angels and spirits of departed loved ones. One of the reasons they believe this is because they often see young children stare, smile or coo at a particular spot in a room as if someone invisible was actually standing there. On occasion the baby may even lift its arms to that spot.

This staring, smiling or cooing at something or someone invisible to the adult eye is something many babies do. Many parents barely notice it because they think it is just another of those quirky, cute things babies do, but from all I have researched and read on the subject it is clear to me that something incredible may be going on and that babies do have an innate ability to see angels. And the hundreds of parents who have written to me about their babies would agree with me. They know that their babies are seeing things that we adults cannot.

Here are some quotes from just some of the many emails I have received on this subject:

I believe children can see angels. My six-week-old son looks at the wall and starts to smile and shake his hands like he is trying to wave at someone. I don't know but I like to think it is my grandparents watching over him. I never feel scared because I know that whoever or whatever he is seeing is someone or something that loves him.

Gordan

There are times my three-month-old stares at the ceiling, follows something with her eyes and has a huge smile on her face. This does not happen all the time and there are no specific times.

Jill

I believe my two-month-old can see angels. I think she can see my mother. I lost her in 2004 and got very emotional when I had my baby because she wasn't there with me, enjoying the experience. I believe that my angels knew this and sent my mother as my daughter's guardian angel and that my daughter sees her all the time. She stares up and her eyes move around and she smiles. She actually smiles more in her sleep and at 'nothing' than she smiles at me or my husband.

Donna

I could fill an entire book with beautiful stories like this about babies and their angels. I never get tired of reading them or hearing them because each and every one makes me feel happy. I can sense the love, joy and wonder these new parents are feeling as they observe their babies experiencing life in this way. I'm prompted to recall many wonderful memories of my own children when they were babies. My son would frequently pull away from feeding and staring at me to smile at the wall behind me. I'd try and get his focus back to me but it was a lost cause. Obviously, the wall behind was much more interesting. My daughter would also behave in a similar way. She'd be sitting up in her cot and lose all interest in her toys and become absorbed by a spot on the ceiling above her. Sometimes she would babble and reach out to it. Again, I would try to get her attention back to me or the toys but again I was considered far less interesting. It's a weird experience, feeling jealous of a wall or ceiling!

The great majority of the parents and carers who send in their stories on this subject don't claim to have seen angels with halos and wings, but the unexplained behaviour of their babies has convinced them that the babies are definitely seeing something, and this something is entertaining or comforting them in some way. Never are there any indications that their babies are in any way distressed by the experience. Indeed, as this story by Beatrice shows, the opposite is the case.

White sky

Last year my eighteen-month-old daughter and I had quite the experience. I was trying to get her into her car seat and as usual she was making it very difficult for me. Ever since she was born she had been a very demanding child, very wilful, and there were times when I was close to losing it. This was one of those times. I was in a hurry and there was someone waiting to get into my parking spot – so the pressure was on. My daughter, however, had other plans. She got very excited and started flapping her arms. She was pointing over my shoulder to the sky and said, 'Big angels. Look, sky.' I don't know why but something made me look in the direction of her pointed finger. I thought I'd see a bird or a balloon or something passing over but there was nothing, just a very white sky. I finished strapping her into her car seat and she kept saying over and over again, 'Big angels.' I told her to stop making things up but she wouldn't let it drop and kept saying it as we drove home.

I decided to just ignore it. If nothing had changed after that incident I wouldn't have written to you because I've never believed in angels or anything like that, but I'm starting to change my mind now because I have started to notice that my daughter has become more loving and cuddly since this happened. She has always been the type of baby that would rather be put in her crib and left alone than be rocked. She also gave hugs and kisses infrequently. Now, she just loves on us all the time! I don't know if she saw an angel, but I'm drawn to the idea.

Beatrice's story is a good example of the letters and emails I get from parents who find talk of angels rather unsettling at first, but then it all begins to feel familiar and comforting. Many tell me that a lovely peace descends over their children when they see angels and this stops them worrying about how strange it might seem.

The huge and well-documented number of stories about angels and babies has convinced me that we are all born with the eyes to see angels. I am also convinced that we don't have to lose this ability and at any point in our lives we can reconnect with it. Trouble is, from the age of three, when toddlers start to communicate with words, they are likely to find out that their parents can't see what they have been seeing – and often don't believe what they are saying anyway – and this lack of belief and trust by the people they love and rely on the most can lead to self-doubt. Self-doubt is the enemy of psychic development and herein begins a process called conditioning. When children are told at the most receptive stage in their young lives that some things are real and some things, like spirits, are not, their instinct is to please their parents. If they are told over and over again that what they are seeing isn't real they will, in time, lose their ability to see angels and often their memoires of heaven as well.

Instead of feeling anxious, I urge all parents and carers to delight in the fact that their infants can see angels, almost as soon as they are born. I urge them to celebrate that wonderful connection. It is the most natural thing in the world for babies to see spirits or angels. As this second story from Anne-Marie shows, every baby is a miracle straight from heaven.

With the other babies

When my youngest daughter, Melissa (now twenty-one), was very little – I can't remember exactly how old but I am guessing about twenty months, certainly under two – I asked her where she was before she was born. I did this deliberately to see what she would say. I didn't tell her what 'born' meant, and I did it when I felt she would still be young enough to remember, but old enough to have the speech to express herself. She answered 'with the other babies'. That was all. But she didn't look puzzled by the question.

The unique and very special bond between babies and angels isn't just created when they are kissed by their guardian angel at birth; it exists before they are born or even thought of by their parents and continues to exist as they journey forward in their lives and become toddlers, infants and children.

Before leaping forwards with stories about angels and children, I'd first like to tell you to forget anything you may have heard or read previously about so-called crystal or indigo children, or children born with unique psychic powers that set them apart from all the rest. According to some 'new age' experts, these children are sent from the world of spirit to save us from ourselves, and a number of books and websites have grown up around this concept, some of which provide checklists and personality tests to see if your child or a child you know falls into this unique group. Personality traits include such things as wisdom beyond their years, heightened sensitivity and imagination and so on.

While I have great sympathy with the idea that we can learn from our children and grow up again alongside them, I have no sympathy with the idea of a so-called select group of children chosen for this sacred purpose. In my opinion, all children have been kissed by angels, and every child is a blessing sent from heaven to bring hope and a sense of possibility and positive transformation to the world. The next two stories illustrate this well. They both got my attention and I'm including them right here because until their angel encounter, neither of the children involved demonstrated any psychic potential whatsoever. I'll start with Katy's story:

Recovery position

Sam is my seven-year-old son. I'd be the first to admit that he's a bit of a troublemaker. I think he spends more time outside the classroom than inside it at school. He's calmed down a lot recently, though, and I'm wondering if an experience he had last month might be the reason. It was quite a nice day and I sent him outside in the garden to play while I did some chores. I was busy ironing when I heard a scream. I rushed outside and saw Sam lying on his side. The rascal had been trying to 'tightrope walk' on our back wall again, even though I told him again and again not to because our back wall is too high for him to fall safely. There was blood on the side of his head and he looked really out of it. I immediately phoned for an ambulance. I told him to keep absolutely still. I don't know much about first aid but I did know that moving him might make things worse.

It was an agonizing half an hour before we made it to hospital. When we got there the doctors praised me for putting him in the recovery position. When I told them I had found him like that they told me he must have been very fortunate to fall and land on his side in the recovery position. If he'd landed in any other way his injuries could have been far worse. It was only when we got home the following day – when Sam got the all clear – that he told me something that sent shivers down my spine.

Sam – and although he's a rascal, he's never been one to make things up – told me that when he fell down he had fallen on his back first but there was a woman beside him called Hannah and she gently pushed him over onto his side. I asked him what this woman looked like and he told me she had long blonde hair, a lovely smile and a very large staining-type birthmark on her cheek. I just could not take it all in. Hannah had been my best friend from junior school to senior school and a few years afterwards. We'd been inseparable until she was killed in a car crash. We'd always talked about how cool it would be to both become mums at the same time and it still brings a tear to my eye when I think that she never got the chance. Hannah had blonde hair and a large facial birthmark, but when she smiled you didn't even notice it. As far as I know I have never told Sam about her, because it's a painful memory for me.

Sam's coming up to his eighth birthday now. He looks at me like I'm crazy when I ask him about Hannah and tells me he can't remember anything. I like to think, though, that she is watching over him as if he was her own.

This next angel-and-child story sent in by Jill is also revealing. There are so many things about it that are hard to explain away. See what you think.

Captured together

I had to write to you and share this story because I know you will like it and I hope others will too. It happened when I moved into my new house five years ago after the death of my husband. He was in the army so you'd have thought that I would have been prepared for the possibility of his death, but nothing prepares you. The first six months were hell. I lost my will to live and it's only because my husband's parents lived close by and could help with the kids that I pulled through.

Anyway, my eldest, Sasha, who was six at the time, was looking through some old picture albums that belonged to my husband. They'd been buried somewhere in the attic in our old house and she had never seen them before. I wanted to put them away for when she was older, but she really wanted to look through them. As we were flicking through the pages celebrating my husband's birth and early school years, Sasha put her finger on one photo and told me she knew who that was. I looked at the photo and it was a picture of my husband – aged twelve at the time – and another boy. She told me in a very matter-of-fact way that the boy's name was Simon and that he came to visit her all the time.

I told her that was impossible because this photo was taken years ago and Simon would be around my age now – and certainly not twelve – but she insisted. This kind of talk worried me because Sasha was not the kind of child to make things up. Perhaps she was mistaken, but she insisted it was him and that he first came to chat with her when her dad died. I asked where she had met him and she told me the first time she saw him was at the funeral. After that he used to come and talk to her in the playground at school, and sometimes he'd sit on her bed at night and read stories to her. I asked her if she thought this was a bit strange, that a boy with no home to go to was following her around, and she just looked at me and sighed. It was as if she was saying there was nothing wrong at all with what she was telling me and I was the one who needed to understand.

I didn't want to upset Sasha – and thought it was just an imaginary friend – so just went along with it, but in my head I was thinking about calling my GP for advice. Fortunately, my husband's parents came over one evening so I decided to talk to them first. Out of curiosity I asked them who the boy in the photo was. They told me his name was Simon and he had died in a canoeing accident just a few days after that photo with my husband was taken. There is no way that Sasha could have known who this boy was.

My mother-in-law, who believes in angels, told me that Sasha was experiencing something incredible and there was absolutely nothing for me to worry about. I should let things be. And as others often are, she was absolutely right because Sasha has grown up into the most beautiful, sensitive, caring and together teenager you could imagine. She can't remember anything about Simon now but treasures that photo of him and her father together. When I ask her why that photo in particular she tells me it is because her dad looks so carefree in it, and she likes to think that wherever he is he isn't lonely because he is with his friend in spirit.

And just a couple more angel-and-child stories before we move on; this first was sent to me by Rachael.

I believe you

My sister asked me to pick up my nephew Edward, age four, from school. Having picked him up I told him I was reading a book about angels and that I believed in them. I asked him if he had ever seen one and he told me he had and it was a bright, bright light in his bedroom. I asked him what colour it was and he said it was yellow. I told him I believed him.

And this one comes from Jackie:

The tooth fairy

I have four children. My middle daughter is ten years old. Her name is Sonia. Last year when she was nine, she told me one morning that she had seen the tooth fairy even though she didn't have a tooth for her. I didn't think much more of it until I read one of your books. I asked her what she looked like and she said the fairy had white sparkles around her and brilliant white wings and a high-pitched voice. She can't really remember what she said to her but she is still adamant this is what she saw. She never tells anyone because they won't believe her but I think I do. Could this have been an angel? I lost a baby last year due to having an abortion, and I like to think maybe this was my baby, but if not will my baby be an angel or with the angels?

I wrote back to tell Jackie I had no doubt her baby was with the angels, watching over and loving her. I also congratulated her on the inspiring way she was speaking to her daughter about angels – nurturing her connection with the world of spirit, instead of ignoring or repressing it and making her doubt it as many adults do.

141

Children have such a receptive, unquestioning attitude towards the invisible world that they can often see what we adults cannot. Unfortunately, as they get older their refreshing and open spirituality gets repressed by the disbelief of those around them and by peer pressure and fear of ridicule. It doesn't have to be that way, though, and I really hope just reading this book will not only encourage you to nurture your child's connection with the unseen, as Rachel did with her nephew, but also help you relive your own childhood and see the world once again with the eyes of a child.

Stories about angels and children always capture the imagination, but something that surprised me when I started writing my angel books is just how many teenagers got in touch with me to discuss or share their angel beliefs and experiences. I guess, in hindsight, I should not have been so surprised because leaving childhood behind can be a scary and unsettling time these days, with hormones, peer pressure, constant exams and expectations to deal with, not to mention the menacing reality of global recession, terrorism, crime and war. In times past young people may have found comfort in religion or in the words of wisdom from grandparents and neighbours but with religion on the decline and families and communities breaking down, increasing numbers of teenagers are seeking comfort in the belief that angels are watching over them.

The stories sent in to me by young adults are all unique, but one striking feature they have in common is that each encounter with the divine offers the recipient a much needed dose of hope, comfort and security in an uncertain and difficult world. I'd like to illustrate this point with this moving story sent to me by Luke about his teenage years.

The best decision I ever made

I'm thirty-two now with a good job, a lovely wife and a baby on the way. Every morning when I wake up I count my blessings because if I hadn't turned my thinking and my life around when I was seventeen I might not even be alive. You see, when I was a teenager I was heading down a very dangerous and dark road. I'd like to tell you about it.

It all started when I turned sixteen. Up until then I'd been quite a good lad. My mum raised me and my three brothers on her own and we are all taught the difference between right and wrong. But then this new family moved next door to us on our estate and I started to hang out with Zack and Conner, the two eldest boys. They were a few years older than me and seemed so cool and tough and they accepted me as one of them. Life felt edgy and exciting when I was around them. I was part of something. I wasn't out there on my own any more.

I remember coming home one day feeling very depressed. After months – no, years – of having this huge crush on a girl in my class I had finally plucked up the courage to ask her out. Come to think of it this was probably the first time I had ever talked to a girl. Coming from a family of four boys I didn't know how to talk to girls so I just didn't. It took every ounce of my courage to ask her out but she told me straight that I wasn't her type, but she'd be happy to be my friend. I felt like I'd been punched in the stomach.

My mum sensed something was wrong when I came home and told me that I was young and I would meet someone great someday. That just made me feel worse. I went next door to hang out with my new friends instead and to cheer me up they suggested going into town and having a laugh. That laugh included some shoplifting and lots of drinking. The adrenaline rush made me forget all about my broken heart.

Several months down the line I was spending almost all my free time hanging out with my new mates. I think Mum knew that something was going on when my grades nose-dived at school, but with a full-time job and four of us to run after I don't think she had the time to think things through. And then came the day when my life changed.

Zack and Connor decided it was time for me to go on a joyride with them. We broke into a car and for half an hour or so it was wild. So wild that we crashed into another car and the next thing I remember is waking up in hospital with my mother sitting beside me.

What happened next is pure magic. I looked at my mum and plain as day I saw a figure standing behind her with its hands resting gently on her head. It was dressed in white and it was crying. I say 'it' because it could have been male or female. Then when Mum noticed I'd opened my eyes it vanished. I could tell that Mum had been crying. Her eyes were so red and at that moment I knew that I never wanted to see my mum like this again. I was going to pull myself out of this black hole for her sake. She didn't deserve this.

To this day I don't know who or what that transparent figure was standing behind Mum or whether it was seeing the figure or my mum in pieces that shocked me into turning my life around, but whatever happened I made the best decision of my life that day. I decided from that moment on to make my mum proud of me. And by making that decision I discovered a self-belief and confidence inside me that simply hadn't been there before. I got my head down at school and became the first member of our family ever to attend university. I made my mum cry again when I got my degree – but in a good way this time.

An angel encounter was also the catalyst for transformation in Bess's story, below.

The reflection

I'm nineteen years old and until earlier this year I hated the way that I looked. It got so serious at one point that my parents sent me to a therapist and I was diagnosed with body dysmorphia. I guess you could compare dysmorphia in some way to someone who wants a sex change. I have never felt comfortable in my own body. It's worse than that, though, because unlike them I didn't have any idea what I should look like. Every time I saw myself in the mirror I would have to take a deep breath. I saw something alien, disgusting.

I would see my eyes as bulging and surrounded by lines and bags. The top part of my face would look tiny in comparison to the bottom half. Wearing a hat would make me feel very uncomfortable and even if it was freezing cold I wouldn't wear one, because I'd be scared it would draw attention to my huge jaw. My lips would always look distorted, with the lower one so much thinner than the top one. I didn't think my neck was long enough – it was like I didn't have one.

145

My eyebrows were the wrong shape, however much I plucked them, and my skin was always peeling and dry and crumpled.

I can't remember a time when I felt comfortable in my own skin. As early as the age of five or six I remember being in the playground and feeling too ugly to belong with the other children. When I got older I wished I could wear a burka to hide my face. I didn't want to inflict my grotesque features on anyone else. I didn't have enough confidence to make friends and was bullied for being such a loner.

In my early teen years I developed an eating disorder. I've never had a weight problem, but food was something that I could control and losing weight made me feel that at least I was succeeding with something in my life. I also had this obsession with washing myself and on very bad days would shower ten or twenty times. I'd scrub and scrub myself until my skin was sore and bleeding. Somehow seeing the blood released the tension inside me and this is when my self-harming began. I started to cut my arms and the inside of my thighs, places where no one would notice.

It wasn't until I was eighteen that my life started to change for the better. I was walking past a shop and as usual the reflection I saw fascinated and disgusted me. I looked fat and ungainly and horrible, but then as I walked on I saw my reflection morph into something astonishingly beautiful. It stopped me dead in my tracks. I saw this beautiful woman looking back at me. She smiled at me and held out her hand. She was just perfect. I was mesmerized and stood there with my hands pressed against the window gazing at her for several minutes until a shop assistant came to the window to replace a mannequin. The shop assistant smiled and waved at me. She looked so friendly that I smiled and waved back before moving on.

Walking home that day was a whole new experience. I literally felt like I was walking on air. Was it possible that the woman I saw in the reflection was me or had I seen my guardian angel? Either way, I felt truly blessed. Everything changed from then on. I wasn't cured overnight, and my eating disorder took the longest to heal, but slowly and steadily I turned a corner and started to like the woman I see every day in the mirror.

Although it happened in a different way, James, whose story is below, also believes his life was saved by angels.

An angel carried me

I want to tell you my story. I didn't see an angel, talk to one or feel one but I'm sure an angel saved my life. It happened last winter when I went out with my brother and a bunch of my friends to celebrate my birthday. It was freezing cold and I thought it would be fun to run across a lake that had frozen over. Being the daredevil I am I dashed into the centre. The ice held firm and it felt great. My brother – always the sensible one – was screaming obscenities at me and begging me to come back. I just laughed back at him and called him a chicken and then I heard the ice crack.

In a split second I realized that I was in big trouble. My brother realized it too and shouted at me to rush back as fast as I could. I started to head back but every time I moved more ice cracked around me. I knelt down to crawl but it made little difference. The ice cracked some more and I plunged in. I have never known true fear till that moment. I thought I was going to die.

At first I didn't feel the cold. It felt like I was hallucinating but then the cold hit me like a truck. I could see my brother trying to get to me but it was impossible. I shouted at him to stay back. There was no point two of us dying. Mercifully, he listened to me and I saw him frantically using his mobile phone.

For about five minutes I struggled to keep my head above water but eventually I got so exhausted I gave up and started to sink down. This sounds weird to say now but at the time it felt very peaceful and calm, kind of good. I didn't feel cold, just completely relaxed. What happened then is incredible. I just felt this pair of arms push me up to the surface of the water and then from underneath push me along, breaking the ice along the way. In a matter of seconds I had done the impossible. I was at the side of the lake and being pulled out of the water by my brother. 'How did you do that?' He was just as amazed as I was by what happened.

I still haven't got the faintest idea how I got out of the water that day, but after reading one of your books I think it is very possible that an angel carried me. I can't think of any other explanation. Something not of this world intervened and I am convinced I have an invisible protector or guide watching over me. This doesn't mean, though, that I'm going to do anything stupid or reckless again. I don't ever want to feel such fear again. It's made me realize how precious my life is. I'm not scared of dying but I'm scared of dying before I have lived, if you know what I mean.

Andrew's story isn't as dramatic, but the effect on his life was just as astonishing.

A steady hand

My angel experience occurred when I was somewhere between fifteen and sixteen years old. I was in secondary school at the time and struggling with my studies because I have dyslexia and my school wasn't providing the special needs facilities that I needed to help me cope. I was in my religious-studies class feeling frustrated and worthless again because I couldn't handle the assignment I'd been set. In our class we had a seating plan, with three rows of tables — four tables within each row. I was sitting beside the aisle, in the middle row. Across the aisle was a metal cupboard containing exercise books; it was no more than three to four feet away from me.

I was trying and failing to write something down when I got the sensation that something was next to me (in the aisle on my right side). Obviously there was nothing there. I continued writing. Then, I felt the extremely strong sensation of a warm hand resting on my right shoulder . . . so strong that I had to look in that direction. Nothing was there; and it couldn't have been anyone behind me, as there is at least two feet of space between each row. The 'person' seemed to me to be possibly be five feet seven, or slightly taller. You must remember that nothing was visible to me at this time — it was my sixth sense. But that hand on my right shoulder felt like a real hand, not an energy . . . a real hand!

The next day when my teacher marked my assignment she told me it was the best piece of work I had ever handed in to her. I don't know why but I told her about what I had experienced in class. She didn't laugh or tell me off, she just smiled and asked me if the experience had made me feel calm and happy. I told her it had and she told me that it had to have been my guardian angel then. It meant a lot to be taken seriously by her and my work improved from that day onwards. I got eight GCSE passes, with a B grade in religious studies.

Whenever young people like Andrew write to me, or I read stories about children and young adults, I draw great inspiration from the way they talk about angels and approach the whole subject. Angel encounters give them such courage and self-belief and their open-mindedness and lack of doubt or mistrust is something we adults can all learn from. I truly believe that the way to nurture our young people is to judge less and listen more and to stop trying to suppress their spontaneity, enthusiasm and open-mindedness and to encourage them to look within and around them for answers, comfort and inspiration. To show them by our own inspiring example of love, trust and open-mindedness, that there is something more than the material world and it is this something more which gives our lives reason, purpose and meaning.

As you've seen so far in this chapter, angels are within and around us from our birth – perhaps even before that – through our childhood and to our teenage years. And the comfort and protection doesn't stop then – it continues into our adult years and our old age. Although we may not be as able to see our angels, or trust in them as readily as children do, they are still with us, waiting for us to notice and understand them. And they are never closer to us than when we are faced with new challenges. This is something Mel, age fifty-one, discovered when the last of her children left home.

My baby girl

I'd like to tell you about something that happened to me on the day my baby girl moved out. She'd been my life for the last nineteen years. I missed her so much, especially when I went shopping. I missed our chats when she came home from school and late-night cups of cocoa when my husband had gone to bed. I missed everything, basically. My heart felt so lonely. It didn't help that my friends kept telling me I should be happy. They said it was my time now, time for me and my husband to act like teenagers again. Thing is, I didn't want to act like a carefree teenager again. I wanted to act like a mum. Being a mum was all I knew. My son had left home five years before my daughter. It had hurt then but with a son you kind of think you are going to lose them anyway. It felt very different with my daughter. She had always been my baby girl.

The day she moved out, I just sat in my living room. It felt odd – emotionally strange. Here at last was that time I had always said I wanted for myself, but what had I really wanted it for? It wasn't the same for my husband. His life wasn't that much different at all. He still had his job and his routines. I didn't know what I was going to do with myself. I sat and cried and cried. It was close to lunchtime when I stopped sobbing. I kept checking my phone to see if she had texted but there was nothing. I thought about calling her to check she was OK, but I knew that wasn't the right thing to do.

Then I fell asleep and I had this stunning dream. In my dream I was in a green field and I was holding a magnificent kite in my hands. I was having a good time flying it and admiring it as it jumped and turned in the sky but then it started to pull at the string, making it difficult for me to hold on. Eventually, it reached the end of its string and I had to decide what to do. The kite was flying high and demanding more freedom. It wanted to go higher and I was stopping it. I stood on my tiptoes to try to give it more height and raised my hand high up into the sky. Then I stopped holding it and let the string slip through my fingers. The moment of release had come and I watched the kite soar triumphantly into the blue sky, gleaming in the sunshine until it was just a pinpoint on the horizon.

When I woke up I could not stop thinking about my dream. I remembered how sad I felt when I let the kite go but also how excited and proud to see it fly solo. In an instant flash of recognition I realized that my dream was a symbol of where I was that day – standing on my tiptoes and reaching towards the sky with the string of the kite in my fingers, not wanting to let go. But it was time for me to let my daughter go. It was time to let a new relationship with her grow.

My dream didn't just give me the strength to cope with my feelings of loss; it also gave me some fantastic ideas about what I was going to do now. I used to work as an illustrator for a greetings-cards company and the brilliant and vital colours in my dream made me want to reach for a paper and pen and start sketching. I'm now in the process of setting up my own greetings-cards company, and one of the first cards I'm going to design is for parents whose children have left home. On the card will be a picture of a person letting go of a beautiful kite. My husband is an accountant and he is taking care of the business side. It's very exciting.

As for my baby girl, she has settled in well at college. I did the right thing not to call her that day because she really needed the freedom to grow. She's just started her third year now and we are the best of friends. It's certainly not the same as before — it's different, but it's a good different, if you know what I mean.

Another story about letting go comes from Kate, forty-two.

Fade to grey

I feel a bit silly writing to you about this because it's not a big deal really. It happens to everyone but discovering my first grey hairs at the age of thirty-eight was a huge shock to me. I was single at the time and had just gone through a messy divorce. I didn't have any kids, but I was still hoping to be a mother, and that grey hair made me feel very depressed. I'd always looked young for my age and liked the way men looked at me, but it felt as if I had changed from a sexy woman into an old woman in a matter of weeks. Who would date me now?

On top of that stress, I was also finding it harder and harder to keep my body in shape. I was getting more aches and pains than usual and my vision wasn't as sharp as it used to be. I had to face up to the fact that time hadn't stood still and I was getting older. It was a shock.

My first instinct was to rush to the hairdressers and have my hair dyed. Then I signed up with a gym and booked some sessions with a personal trainer. It was while I was at the gym for my second session that I got my wake-up call. I was running on the treadmill and the gym was fairly deserted. Suddenly, I was aware of a little girl standing beside me watching me. She made me feel quite uncomfortable because she just kept standing there. I couldn't turn around and see her properly because I was on the treadmill so I just tried to ignore her. Then she started giggling and I heard her say, 'You're running so fast but not going anywhere.' That was it. She was annoying me now so I stopped the machine and turned around to ask her to leave. But she was gone. I went to the desk and asked the attendant who the little girl was and she told me that children were not allowed into the gym, at any time.

Did I imagine that little girl? I have no idea. She seemed so real. Perhaps she had slipped in without the attendant seeing her – she was a tiny little thing. To this day I have no idea who she was but for the rest of the day what she said to me kept going around and around in my head: 'You're running so fast but not going anywhere.' I realized that she had been right. I was trying to roll back the years, when what I should have been doing was adapting and changing and enjoying the view as I went along.

Don't get me wrong. I'm not giving up and letting myself go, I'm just going with the flow more. I'm learning to be grateful for what I have got and learning that being older does have benefits, like knowing what you want and what you don't want in a relationship, not worrying so much about what other people think and, best of all, not taking yourself so seriously. I've just started dating a man who says I look great for my age, whatever that means. It's early days yet, but we do have a lot of fun together. My new mantra is to have a giggle at myself more often, just like that little girl who stood by me on the treadmill.

As Kate says, getting older is all about learning to adapt and change and this is a good thing. My great-aunt Rose, who was a spiritualist, always used to tell me that the day she had nothing left to learn about herself was the day she would be old. She was in her eighties when she said that. She also used to tell me that you have to keep an open, curious mind about yourself and others throughout your life. One of the themes of this book is people coming to realize something that at a younger age they would not have been ready to understand. In many ways, then, it is about the wisdom of growing up.

Sadly, we live in a world today that often values youth over age and wisdom, but getting older can be a thrilling adventure. Looking at myself in the mirror today, I don't see the young face I used to have any more. I really wish I could have my girlish looks and my radiant skin back, but I would never trade who I am today for who I was twenty or thirty years ago. I wouldn't trade my experiences. I wouldn't want to figure everything out again. The older I am, the happier and wiser I become, because time and experience have helped me value what is important in life and taught me so much about myself. It makes me sad whenever I hear other people talking about how they wish they could turn back the clock, or saying that their school days were the best days of their lives. That is just not true. Self-knowledge is something that cannot be taught. It comes with age. Each individual has to learn it from within. The older you are, the more perceptively you can see yourself and others. And, as Ian, seventy-seven, explains below, that is the deepest inner joy and gift from your angels that you could ever experience.

I can see angels

If you had told me twenty − or forty − years ago I'd be writing to an angel author I would have told you that would never happen. I didn't believe in the supernatural and certainly not in angels, but then something happened to change my mind and my life. That something was the birth of my grandchild, the appropriately named Angela.

When she was born I was starting to feel my age. I never thought I'd get old but it crept up on me unawares. I didn't like the aches and the pains, the physical limitations, and the only bright spot on the horizon was little Angela. I really settled into my role as granddad very well. When my son was growing up I was always so busy with work I never got to spend enough time with him, but when Angela was born I had retired and was ready to play the role of doting granddad. Every weekend I'd call round to spend some time with her so my son and his wife could go out.

When Angela was about five she started to ask me all those 'why' questions, and as any parent or teacher knows, some of the can be tough. I did my best to answer them but when she started asking about God and angels because she had been taught to pray at school, I was at a loss for words. I toyed with the idea of telling her that I didn't believe in those things but then she said, 'I can see angels.'

Thinking it was all a childish game I asked her if her angel was with her now and she closed her eyes and started to move her head from side to side, apparently to get the best view. As far as I know my son and his wife had never spoken to her about angels − and they certainly weren't into meditation − so this was all strange to me.

Eventually she told me, still with her eyes closed, that she could see her angel now.

Something inside me decided to see where all this was going, so I asked her if I could see her angel too. She paused and then said that her angel wanted to know why I wanted to see her. I said I felt left out. She paused again and then said that her angel knew my angel and he'd been waiting a long time to see me.

I kept on asking questions and Angela kept on replying and what impressed me was not so much what she was doing – I know children have imaginary friends – but the depth and insight of what she was saying. Her answers seemed like they were coming from someone closer to my age. She said things like, her angel couldn't help her with everything but she could help her cope better and that her angel did not hug her but did let her know that she was loved. Eventually Angela clearly wearied of the conversation and opened her eyes. She gave me such a wonderful hug. She told me that she loved my wrinkles very much.

Everything changed for me that day. I don't know if Angela really saw angels but I can't think of any other explanation for the wisdom and insight of her answers. In the years since – Angela is twenty-six and about to become a mum herself now – I have come to think of that angel as some aspect of her intuition or, as you say in your books, the angel within. She made me realize that there was an angel inside me too, a well of love and wisdom, waiting to get acquainted with me. Watching Angela talk to her angel reminded me to talk to my own. And once I started doing that I became a much happier person than I ever was when I was younger, more dynamic and fit. I learned to appreciate things more. I learned that I didn't have all the answers. I learned that there is far more to this world than meets the eye. I can honestly say that with every passing year I feel happier.

Refocusing on this chapter's theme of angels walking with us through the journey of life, this next story sent to me by Katrina, age thirty-two, spans the generations – great-grandmother, grandmother, mother and grandchild. It shows once again that whenever there is belief, trust and love there are always angels.

Angel babies

I have never seen an angel but I have always believed in them, and have had many, many encounters where I believe an angel has been at work so I thought I would share some of these with you.

My mum has developed a strong belief in angels over recent years. I was certainly not aware of her teaching us about angels as we grew up as children, although I have always, for as long as I can remember, believed that my great-grandmother – who died the same day that I was born – is looking out for me. Every time things haven't gone quite to plan I have prayed to her for help and guidance, and likewise have believed that she has protected me in potentially dangerous situations. I am thirty-two now and my belief in angels is stronger than ever.

When I had my first car at eighteen I took it for a drive along the motorway. I turned off onto an uphill slip road, still travelling very fast and not realizing that at the top of the slip road was a junction with free-flowing, fast-moving traffic crossing in front of me. I must have been travelling at seventy mph. As soon as I saw the traffic I did an emergency stop and I have absolutely no idea how my car stopped in time as I braked so late. But my car stopped on the correct side of the junction. I was terrified and very shaken up, but at that time, and still, I believe that my guardian angel helped me to stop my car.

When I was twenty-five I had a pink, old-style VW Beetle, which was my pride and joy! It was in pretty poor shape but somehow deemed to be roadworthy and I used to drive it everywhere. One day on my way home from work, I came off a roundabout and heard a loud noise as though something had fallen out of the bottom of the car onto the road. At the same time, my steering wheel locked up, as did the brakes, so I had no way of steering or of stopping. I was travelling at around thirty mph and was terrified that I would crash as there was no other way to stop the car. I have no idea — nor does the AA man, garage mechanic or anyone seem to know — how I managed to stop that car as everything had literally locked up. All I did was pull on the steering wheel with both hands as hard as I could and push my foot as hard as was humanly possible onto the brake pedal, which didn't feel like it moved, to be honest, and the car stopped about two inches from the wall of a busy pub. Once again I believe that my guardian angel was there to protect me. I don't see any other explanation.

In 2006 I fell pregnant and was absolutely overjoyed as being a mum was what I had always wanted more than anything. Very sadly, this was an ectopic pregnancy which resulted in the loss of one of my tubes and the surgery caused damage to the opposite ovary. My husband and I didn't know whether or not we would be able to conceive again because of the surgery and consequent damage.

My grandmother, who was like a mother to me and one of my favourite people in the world, had always said that she wasn't planning on 'going anywhere', i.e. passing away, until she saw me have a baby. It was around this time that my husband and I got our first puppy. Sadly, shortly after the ectopic pregnancy she was diagnosed with stomach cancer and had surgery to remove part of her stomach. Once she was back at home recovering from surgery, she phoned me on a Sunday evening and asked me about the puppy. Then she said, 'So you have your baby now', told me she loved me and we ended the call. The following day she passed away.

Since my grandmother's death, whenever I feel unsure, sad, or need comfort, I always see magpies, which I used to look at in her garden with her when I was growing up. I believe these magpies are a sign from my grandmother that she is still with me. I can also smell the scent I always associated with my nan at times when I'm feeling sad, so this enhances my belief. Oddly, my smoke alarm went off on the anniversary of her passing, at exactly the same time she passed away. Our smoke alarm never goes off without any reason, although this could have been a technical fault, granted.

The following February I fell pregnant and went on to have a beautiful little boy, Wayne, who many people have now told me looks like 'he knows more than he is letting on' or 'he has been here before', which I think is probably true. The birth of Wayne was lengthy but I somehow got through it with just gas and air. He was also born with knot in his umbilical cord and with it around his neck. The midwife said that it was a miracle he was born without any complications. As I sat holding Wayne for the first time, the first thing I saw when I looked out of the window in the delivery room was magpies on the grass. I believe that my nan was with me that day, supporting me and protecting both me and Wayne.

When Wayne was tiny he used to stare at the end of his crib and coo and try and reach up, and I have always liked to believe that this was perhaps an angel, or perhaps my nan or my great-nan coming to visit and protect him.

Wayne is now twenty months old and very recently he stared at a photo, that has always been there, of my husband's late father, who Wayne has never met or been told about. He pointed to the picture and said quite clearly, 'Ganddad Dave', which is exactly what his cousins used to call him. My friend was with me and actually asked me who Granddad Dave was as she didn't know the history, so I know that he definitely said it for her to have recognized it clearly! The only explanation I have is that Granddad Dave has visited Wayne, and I am so glad that both he and my nan have been able to see and communicate with Wayne.

Sadly, in May this year I had a miscarriage, which has been devastating as I would love for Wayne to have a brother or sister, not to mention the loss of another child. I take great comfort in the thought, or hope, that my nan is taking care of my angel babies, as I always call them, and that that was perhaps the reason why it was her time to pass away when she did.

In fact, part of the reason for me writing you this ever-increasing email is that I have been taught to look out for signs from angels by way of music, dreams, thoughts, etc., by my mum and I wasn't planning on buying a book for myself today. I went to the shop to buy a book for my husband. I saw your book on the shelf and the title drew me in. As I walked away from the book, there were only two copies left, but something in me would not let me leave the shop without it! I have read up to page 83 in one sitting, and have already taken great comfort from the stories shared in the book. I believe that my buying the book today was the work of my angels, to help me through the grieving process with the miscarriage and to reinforce that they are with me still.

Katrina mentions signs or angel calling cards in the final part of her email, which ties in well with the next chapter, where we'll take a look at these and other divine prompts in much greater detail. For now, I hope her story, along with Trisha's, below, will remind you that even in life situations where it is hard to imagine any comfort at all, such as the loss of a child or loved one, it is still possible to feel the loving touch of angel.

Empty cradle, full heart

There is no tragedy on earth, I believe, greater than the death of a baby. Ashley lived for just two days after he was born. It was like a rip through my soul, but just before he breathed his last he did something extraordinary, and it never fails to comfort me in the dark and lonely times when I ache for him. As he was placed in my arms for the final time, he looked at me with such intense love and understanding. This was something of a miracle, because until then his eyes had barely opened for more than a flicker. Then, before dying peacefully, he looked above my head for several seconds. Theresa, it was a look of such joy, hope and wonder, the memory of it is forever burned into my heart.

Doctors may know why his eyes unexpectedly opened before he died, but I don't care what they have to say. All I know is that my son spoke to my heart and soul that day and without words he told me that there was a loving angel waiting to comfort him and take him back to the other side.

The loss of a baby through miscarriage, stillbirth, cot death or any reason or under any circumstances is devastating. Dreams are shattered and parents have to deal with the loss of their hopes for the future, as well as the loss of a child. I hope stories like Trisha's will show that every baby who has died is just a cloud away. It was just not their time to take their place in this world. Perhaps they chose to give up this life and be reborn in spirit as a guardian angel watching over those who longed to see them on earth. Or perhaps, as I like to think, they just needed to linger a while longer in the love, comfort and joy that is life in spirit. For whatever reason, as difficult and painful as such experiences are to live through, they remind us poignantly that from cradle to beyond the grave, whether times are good or bad, our angels are always watching over and waiting for us. We truly are never alone.

Never alone

Life is a journey that can certainly bring us many challenges, and at times they can seem hard to bear, but this journey is also a pilgrimage and a sacred adventure. Sure, each one of us will face obstacles and countless changes of direction along the way.

Many of us fear these changes, especially when we are young and see the world in black and white, but I hope these stories have shown that change, even when it seems painful and harsh, is essential for us to learn and grow emotionally and spiritually. In fact, it is change which gives life its richness, depth and colour and it is change which makes us feel vibrant, youthful and alive, whatever age we may be. A person is old only when they close their minds and their hearts to the possibility of change and the possibility of discovering something new and magical within and around them.

You see, everything we need for our journey through this life can be found in the angels within and around us. During times of crisis and turmoil our angels can often seem very far away, but if we listen to the inner calling of our hearts and look for what is good and beautiful around us, we will be able to find our angels, and these angels will guide us through life's mysteries.

It is a blessing to know that we are never alone and our angels are always with each and every one of us, offering comfort and hope and guidance in every age and stage of our lives. And, as we'll see later, it is also a blessing to know that our angels will be with us when the time comes for us to take our last breath, when we can face the greatest change of all and are reborn into the world beyond. The journey of our life on earth may have ended, but in the unseen world, our spiritual journey continues and the end is just the beginning.

CHAPTER 6

Heaven on Earth

Spiritual love is a position of standing with one hand extended into the universe and one hand extended into the world, letting ourselves be a conduit for passing energy.

Christina Baldwin

In the previous chapters we've seen how angel encounters can transform a person's life for ever by reminding them during times of crisis and pain that they are not alone and this life here on earth is not all that there is. There is an invisible world of love, peace and spirit, which some call heaven, and it is from this world that we are born and, when the time comes for us to pass over, we will return to that world. And while we are living here on earth heaven hasn't disappeared. If we open our hearts and minds it is very much alive around and within us. All we need to do is believe.

With all the bad news that we are confronted with every day heaven seems a good place to ponder and rest our weary minds.

There are so many tragedies in this world. Natural disasters tear families and communities apart. The acts of cruelty and injustice by mankind alone are staggering. Just watching the news and reading the papers is enough to make anyone long for a glimpse of heaven on earth.

In response to that universal longing, I've decided to linger a while longer here with the many different ways angels can reveal themselves to us right here on earth, before moving on in the final chapter to discuss stories of loved ones visiting us in spirit and visions of the afterlife. I hope this chapter will make it abundantly clear to you that heaven isn't a place that can only be seen when you cross over to the other side. It is possible to glimpse its wonder right here, right now on earth. And when you have glimpsed that wonder, I promise you, your life will never be the same again.

The presence of an angel

If at this point in the book you are still doubting yourself and wondering if you have ever seen an angel, what you are about to read here may give you the answers you've been looking for, or didn't realize you had always been looking for.

First of all, I want to stress again that most angel encounters are not seen; they are felt. There are a number of ways to tell if you are in the presence of an angel. Sometimes an angel will announce its presence with a slight breeze, even when the windows are closed. The breeze is the flutter of their wings. There may be a beautiful scent. You may hear a faint sound, like a bell ringing, or there may be a short-lived high-pitched sound in your ears. I believe this ringing sound is made when angels break from the world of spirit into ours. Sometimes an angelic presence may be accompanied by a flash of light or you may get the feeling that someone is standing behind you but when you turn around there is nobody there. Sometimes there may be a moment of profound insight that seems to come out of nowhere, but by far the most common way to tell if you are in the presence of angels is when you feel an unexpected warm feeling of love and hope rushing over you. This feeling often comes to us in the most unlikely of situations and the only way I can describe it is like having a cup of hot cocoa on a bitterly cold day. When it happens, as Brenda's beautiful story below shows, everything just alters for the better.

A lot of pain

There was a lot of pain in my life and I will never forget the day everything fell apart for me. It was the spring of 2009 and I was forty-three. I was sitting in the living room with my mother. She was chatting away as usual, when suddenly I couldn't hear what she was saying any more. I could see her talking but there was no sound. It all went quiet. All I could hear was my heart beating. I put it down to stress. I'd been working extremely hard, so decided to have a warm bath and an early night. But when I woke up the next morning I felt such heavy pain – not physical pain but emotional pain. I just had this overwhelming feeling of sadness.

Initially I didn't want to deal with it so I tried to pretend it wasn't there. I buried myself in work and accepted every social invitation and doubled up my time at the gym. I went around with a permanent smile on my face but underneath it all I wasn't very well at all. Getting out of bed in the morning was a struggle and during the day I felt as if I was walking uphill with the wind pushing me back.

If I had been honest with myself I would have seen that it had been building up for years. I hadn't been feeling happy for a long time. Almost all my friends had settled down with their partners or were preoccupied with kids. I longed to be in a secure and stable relationship, but it hadn't worked out that way. I did have issues with commitment. Then when I hit forty-two and my oldest and closest friend got pregnant I felt lonelier than ever. I had grown up imagining myself with Mr Perfect and with a perfect child, but all that had become the stuff of dreams. I was middle-aged, single and not a mother. I hadn't even achieved what seemed to come so easily for other women. I felt worthless.

Eventually, it all got too much to hold back and I found myself bursting into tears in the most distressing of places – a packed Tube train early in the morning. There I was sobbing hysterically, surrounded by other commuters who avoided any eye contact and edged away thinking I was crazy. All the hurt rose to the surface. I remembered all the arguments between Mum and Dad before the divorce, how I used to hide in my room until they were over. I remembered the pain of discovering that the man I thought I loved was having an affair. I relived the trauma of my miscarriage. All the hurt and pain just came pouring out, but then something incredible happened. The pain just suddenly lifted and I felt this glow of warmth and love replacing it. It was the most marvellous feeling, like I was being hugged by a gigantic pair of arms.

By the time I got off the train I felt twenty pounds lighter. I felt like I could fly and was tempted to lift my arms and run. Today, the pain hasn't gone completely and memories of it will always remain, but if it ever tries to creep back I have something to replace it with now – memories of that marvellous feeling of warmth and love. Now that I'm finally able to let go of the past I have hope for the future again. Everything in my life feels better.

Earlier in this book, we talked about those 'aha moments' or sudden flashes of intuition and profound insight that can turn lives around. In those stories, angels revealed themselves first to our minds, and after that it is up to us whether we choose to allow them into our hearts, but in stories like Brenda's they reveal themselves directly to our hearts, where there is no resistance to them because our hearts instantly recognize them for what they are. In an instant, pain is replaced by comfort, fear by love and chaos by order.

Now that I've mentioned order, you may have noticed that a recurring theme in many of the stories in this book is order coming out of crisis, certainty arising after doubt, fear turning to hope. Undoubtedly, many people today do feel confused and uncertain and it is all too easy to think that life is chaotic and random, but I'd like to point out that even scientists in recent years are suggesting that there are detectable patterns in chaos. There is nothing random about human DNA, for example, or the intricate designs of a snowflake or a spider's web, just perfect designs where everything has a place, purpose and function. Patterns and an unexplained intelligence without human interference can be seen everywhere in the natural world, in all living things, and this argument leads us to another common way for the reality of heaven on earth to be revealed to us. I have had many letters and emails from people whose lives have been transformed or given a sense of inspiration and certainty by the natural world. This was certainly the case for Elaine on her trip to Florida.

Water ballet

Last summer I went on the trip of a lifetime to Florida with my husband Simon. We were walking along the shores of a coastal river when suddenly four dolphins appeared and started to 'dance' just for us, or so it seemed. A couple of pelicans overhead began to join in and it looked like they were copying the dolphins' movement as they circled and spiralled and dived in and out of the water. Then two manatees started to join in with this water ballet. It was a stunning and unforgettable sight and so perfectly choreographed I half expected a sea lion to appear with a baton conducting them.

Such a sight would have been incredible at any time in our lives but there could have been no better timing than this. We had gone on vacation with heavy hearts, having just lost a dear friend in a brutal mugging. We both felt numbed by the extensive media coverage and increasingly began to feel that we lived in a world where violence and terror were all-encompassing. When we saw our water ballet it was as if the world was saying, 'Don't give up. Look at us – we just keep on dancing through life's ups and downs.' Our hearts and our spirits were restored by that beautiful sight and we returned home determined to survive and thrive, just like the lovely creatures who had danced to the rhythm of life for us.

The natural world was also a source of inspiration and comfort for Mark. Here's his story.

A father's grief

If you had looked into my eyes last year you would have seen a man in anguish. They say eyes are the windows of the soul and mine were broken. I was a broken man because my daughter died. When my wife died they called me a widower but what title should I have when my daughter died? All the people who cared for me cried beside me, but I didn't feel them with me. Then after a few months they stopped talking about my little girl, as if she had been airbrushed out of our lives. I felt lonelier than ever and the phone eventually stopped ringing. My counsellor told me it was nothing to do with me. It was just that people didn't know what to say. I don't think anyone knows what to say to a bereaved parent. People fear death, you see – like it is contagious or something.

My counsellor told me all about the stages of grief: denial, anger, bargaining, depression and finally acceptance. He told me mine was a natural reaction after my unspeakable loss, but reaction is an understatement. Grief is a 'mind, body and spirit' torment that runs through every aspect of your being. Unless you have been through it you cannot ever understand it. Not only is your heart ripped to shreds but nobody tells you about the physical pain. It's like every nerve in your body is exposed and sore. It's hard to breathe. Everything hurts and then there is the fatigue beyond description. Sometimes you wonder how you can feel so much pain and still be alive.

As for the stages of grief I'm expected to go through, is there really any incentive to get to acceptance? Why would I want to get over or accept my child's death? When you lose a part of yourself like that it is something you just can't move forward from. It changes your life and nothing is ever the same again. It can't be the same.

This is as close a description as I can give of how I felt until a few months ago, when I believe my daughter started to speak to me. It began when I spotted what looked like an angel in the clouds. I was walking home when I looked up and saw her there in the clouds before me at the end of the road. It was a perfect bust in profile with her wings outspread in flight. The colours were spectacular, with pastels of lavender, pink and more. To me, this was the most wonderful and magical message I could have received. It lifted my heart for the first time in years and made me smile from the inside out.

I saw the same cloud again the following day. It looked even more perfect than before. And then I saw it for the third day in a row. It had to be more than a coincidence. It had to be my daughter speaking to me, letting me know she was all right.

I told my counsellor what I had seen. He looked a bit scared at first and tried to explain it as my first steps towards acceptance of my daughter's death. I told him that I hadn't accepted her death and that my angel cloud had convinced me she was still very much alive. I attended only one more session after that. My counsellor just didn't want to talk about the angel in the clouds, but for me it was all I wanted to talk and think about.

Today, I'm back at work and in a new relationship with a woman who believes in angels as much as I do. I haven't seen my angel cloud again but the memory of it sustains me. The grief hasn't gone away but it has transformed into something beautiful and peaceful, instead of something ugly and painful.

I thanked Mark for the honest way he shared his experience of brutal grief with me, and for the courage he is showing coming to terms with his loss. I told him he was right to leave his counsellor when he felt ready. His counsellor had helped him deal with his emotional and physical pain, but the only way for him to truly feel whole again was to address his spiritual pain and sense of loss. Mark's angel-cloud sign was the comforting signal he needed to move forward with his life, a life where his daughter is always with him in spirit.

If you ever want to see angels, one of the best places to start is in the natural world. Just look around you. It's one of the simplest and most uplifting ways to boost your spiritual energy. Nature truly is the favourite hiding place of the angels. Have you ever felt the kiss of an angel in a snowdrop or the whisper of angels in the rustling of leaves or a gentle breeze? Has the sight of a rainbow or the stunning shape of a cloud ever taken your breath away? As Carla's story shows, there is a spark of the divine in the natural world, and in all living things.

The peacock

My grandmother and I were very close and when we got the news that she didn't have long to live it really felt like a blow to the heart. I went to visit her the night before she died and she seemed very chatty.

When it was time for me to go she grabbed my hand and told me that she loved me and would always be watching over me when she was gone. On the day of her funeral, we went to my aunt's house for the meal and on the way there we stopped the car to let a peacock cross the road. When it got about halfway it just stopped and looked me straight in the eye. We kept staring at each other until the horn of the car behind us got so loud that the peacock decided to move on.

I didn't think anything of it until a day or so later when a box arrived for me. It couldn't have come at a better time because I was missing Grandma so much and inside there was a perfume-scented letter from her. She must have written it a few weeks before she died. She told me again that she loved me and would be watching over me from the other side. Also inside the letter was a beautiful peacock feather. My grandma said she wanted it to remind me to always celebrate the true beauty of my nature.

I've read many beautiful stories about wild animals, especially birds, somehow communicating messages of hope at just the right time, or offering signs of comfort for those grieving the loss of a loved one. This one sent in by Dawn really caught my eye.

Never gone

It was only when Mum died that I really understood what people meant when they say, 'You don't know what you've got till it's gone.' I loved Mum deeply, but I don't think I ever told her enough. I missed her so much, especially when the kids were at school and my husband was at work. Sometimes I had to stop myself picking up the phone for our usual chat. It didn't seem real that she had gone.

Well, one day her loss really hit me hard and I started crying, wishing I had told Mum how much I loved and valued her when she was alive. I cried and cried and then the doorbell went and I had to dry my tears quickly to answer it. I opened the door but there was no one there. I was just about to close it, thinking it was some kind of prank, when this tiny brown-and-grey bird flew in. It flew around the hall a bit and then sat on the bannister for a few moments, staring at me with brown eyes that reminded me so much of Mum. Then it calmly flew out again. I know it was a message from Mum. I had been crying for her in the morning, wanting to tell her how much she meant to me, and here she was letting me know that she could hear me. I have heard stories about feathers and butterflies, but for me it's a little brown-and-grey bird.

Dawn mentions butterflies in her email and I have read a lot of stories about butterflies – so many in fact that I am inclined to believe that they, along with birds and feathers, may be one of the most common ways for loved ones or angels to communicate with us. Carolyn's story, below, is a lovely example:

The flutter of wings

When my husband died I longed for a sign from him, but three days after his funeral there was nothing. Then one evening this beautiful butterfly appeared out of nowhere in my kitchen. I was mesmerized by it and have no idea how it got in because I had been in the kitchen for several hours and all the doors were shut. I just knew it was my husband whispering words of love to me through the fluttering of its wings and if I had any doubts my cat, Sandy, dispelled them completely. Normally when Sandy sees a butterfly she goes crazy and hunts it down. She's an indoor cat and gets very excited when there are flies or insects in the house, but instead of stalking the butterfly she just sat down and watched it with me. My husband and Sandy had a special bond and I think she knew it was him too.

Nathan works as a funeral director and he's absolutely convinced butterflies are a sign from beyond.

Flying over

In the last few months I have started to notice more than the usual number of butterflies for this time of year. It's also been an extremely busy month or two for my business. Only the other day I saw about five butterflies hovering around one of our coffins. I have always believed that there is some sort of life after death and after reading one of your books I'm more convinced than ever. I just wish the grieving relatives could see things the way I do. A lot of people ask me why I chose to do the job that I do but I always tell them that the job chose me. Five years ago I attended the funeral of a friend who lost his father. They'd been exceptionally close and at the grave-yard I saw this stunningly lovely butterfly land on the coffin. It just lingered there and spread its wings and then it flew over towards me and landed on my head – yes, my head. I knew in that instant that I wanted to do the job I do.

If you've ever seen a bird, insect, butterfly or feather shortly after the death of a loved one, or any time after, and it feels like it is a communication from the world of spirit, please do let me know because, like Nathan says in his email above, the more people hear stories like this the more likely they are to recognize these often ignored messages of love and comfort from beyond the grave. I simply don't know how spirits or angels somehow channel their loving energy into a bird or a butterfly, or even a feather, but it seems that they do. It is an astonishing transformation. All you need to do is ask for a symbol of communication, for the flutter of wings – a whisper in the breeze, a sign in the clouds or any other sign that speaks to your heart.

Butterfly and bird stories are becoming increasingly common, but I've noticed lately a steadily increasing numbers of stories about angels sending messages of heavenly love, comfort and compassion through our beloved pets. Stories like this one sent to me by Dot.

My dog saved my life

When I got my dog I wasn't in a very good place. I'd just given birth to twins and my partner had told me that he wasn't ready for fatherhood yet. Money was tight and I was soon lonely and broke. I also found looking after the twins extremely hard. I felt worthless, sad and lonely. I didn't have a job or a plan and could only see endless days stretching ahead of me on benefits. At times I didn't think I even loved my kids, they reminded me so much of my ex. My life hadn't turned out the way I always thought it would. I couldn't see any way out.

The only bright spot was my sister, Julia. She called round every day to give me some time to myself. One day she came round and told me that she had had a dream and in her dream she had seen me laughing again and the reason I was laughing was because I was playing with a dog. I told her that getting a dog was out of the question because I couldn't even take care of myself and the twins, let alone a dog. Julia looked disappointed but I think she understood.

After Julia had gone I felt more depressed than ever. I'm ashamed to admit it now but I did think about ending it all. It was probably the darkest night of my life ever and I prayed for help. When I woke up the next morning, for reasons I shall never understand, all I could think of was Julia and what she had said about getting a dog. I knew it was impractical but a part of me wasn't listening. It was the part of me that I had forgotten all about. It was the part of me that had always dreamed of having a happy family, a lovely home and a dog. I thought that part of me had long since died but here it was again, confusing me with its optimism and rosy-coloured view of the world.

I'm not sure why – because as I said I was depressed – but I did set off for Battersea to get myself a dog. It was sheer madness, but the urge grew stronger and stronger like I was being led there. Almost as soon as I arrived I was drawn to this Jack Russell Staffy cross. He was so adorable, with brown and white spots, but what really drew me to him were his black eyes. They were like deep pools of love. I looked up to see what his name was and it was Angel. He was eighteen months old and trained but his owner had recently died. I knew this was the dog for me and within a matter of weeks I had brought him home.

Angel worked his magic on me almost the minute he set foot, or should I say paw, in the house. It was like he was always watching me and every time I felt sad he would come up to me or jump up and down as if to say, 'Time to play.' I stopped staying indoors all day because I had to walk him and I felt so much better. So much better in fact that I decided to venture back into the job-hunting business and I found part-time employment at a nursery nearby, which meant I could work and see my twins at the same time.

Angel continues to make my life special every day. When I get up he gives me so much affection, walking him is one of my favourite parts of the day and in the evening when we curl up together on the sofa I feel content. I can't wait for the twins to be older so that they can have fun playing with him and getting to know him. I can honestly say that if my dog hadn't come into my life as he did I might not be here today. I believe all animals, especially dogs, are angels — all breeds and in all shapes and sizes. They love you without condition and always seem to know what you are feeling.

The unconditional love and devotion of a dog can often change a person's life for the better, or, as Dot says in her story, save it. I particularly like her story because the dog at the centre is part Staffordshire bull terrier. Over a century ago this breed was used for pit fighting and this, along with the fact that all too often today Staffies have become a 'status' dog for street gangs, has given it a bad reputation. It's the breed that most often appears in the papers for all the wrong reasons. Stories about dogs attacking their owners or killing babies and children make disturbing reading, but as any vet will tell you, if treated gently, this breed has a good and stable temperament and can make an excellent companion. In the great majority of cases the dog becomes savage because of its treatment by the owner. This may sound dramatic, but from a spiritual perspective I truly believe that in the way we treat our pets, and indeed all animals, nothing short of the direction of our life could be at stake. If we go on treating animals with cruelty, we go on creating a world of suffering for ourselves. What is precious and sacred about life can only grow from honouring and showing compassion to all life forms.

It's not just dogs, of course, that can show extraordinary levels of love, devotion and compassion towards their owners. This next story, sent to me by Linda, features one of the most popular household pets, a cat.

Change of plan

I had no intention of sharing my life with a cat. My ex-husband had a cat allergy and I had been told lots of grisly stories about them – they brought in half-dead animals, they coughed up hair balls and they were only interested in people who fed them. This is how it all started for me.

I was driving home one night and I saw a couple of kids run away from the bins outside my house. I parked my car and took a look around. I couldn't see anything out of the ordinary so started to fumble for my door keys. Then I heard the faintest of mewing. It seemed to be coming from the dustbin. I looked inside and saw a kitten circling around inside. As I said, I'm no cat lover but I can't abide cruelty of any kind, especially against innocent animals who can't defend themselves, so I reached down into the bin and pulled the kitten out. The little mite was freezing cold and obviously starving. I held it up to my chest to warm it and at that moment it pressed a paw onto my chin. My life was never the same after that. This little kitten fired up so much love in me, love I thought I had left behind long ago. Not only did I take the kitten into my heart and into my home but the wonderful love and companionship she gives me prompted me to devote some of my spare time to volunteering at my local RSPCA.

As Linda's experience shows, pets have this seemingly other-worldly ability to change hearts, minds and lives in an instant. Not only can they lift our spirits and heal our pain but they can give our lives meaning, direction and purpose, as this next healing cat story sent in by Monica illustrates so beautifully.

About Charlie

I work as a care assistant in a nursing home for the elderly; have done for more years than I care to remember now. It's heartbreaking to see so many old people spend their final years in isolation. I do my best but I can't be a friend to all of them and some of them have turned so inwards that they don't even want to talk to me. I truly believe that the most serious disease for old people is not cancer or dementia but loneliness and I also believe that pets, especially cats, can be part of the solution. Five years ago I met this lady called Rose. She didn't seem to have anyone, no family and no friends. She had little interest in living. When I tried to interact with her or even feed and wash her she would say over and over again, 'Leave me be, leave me be.' She would spend her days and nights curled up in the foetal position. She had terrible bedsores and would scratch her legs until they bled.

Then this beautiful cat – I think he was Persian, but I'm no cat expect so can't be sure – called Charlie was brought into the home. All the residents fussed over him constantly and he ended up seeking refuge in Rose's bedroom because it was always so quiet with no visitors. Charlie slept on the floor of Rose's room for a few nights and then he started to jump onto her bed. When he was on her bed and Rose tried to curl up her legs he would lie on her stomach so she was forced to stretch out, and when she tried to scratch her legs he would nibble at her hands so she got distracted.

Within two months Rose was sitting up in bed and had stopped scratching herself. The most incredible thing about all this is that she loved the cat so much that she asked staff if she could take care of him and if he could become her cat. There was heated debate about this at the time as lots of residents were fond of him but he had so clearly become Rose's cat that it was decided that Charlie should indeed become known as her cat. When Rose was told of the decision she started inviting other residents to come and visit her in her room to play with Charlie and there was a constant stream of visitors from then onwards.

I've had numerous letters and stories – so many in fact that I often feel I don't give them enough word count in my books – about pets, not just dogs and cats but rabbits, horses, and even ferrets, providing their owners with love and attention at particularly difficult times in their lives. These stories are all proof to me that angels can work with and through animals in much the same way that they can work through other people, through the spirits of lost loved ones and through the natural world, in plants, trees, clouds, oceans and the breeze.

When I was at school the Darwinian notion that life on earth is about the survival of the fittest seemed to be the one that the education system I was in favoured. There seemed no place in this warzone for love, compassion and companionship, but over the years I have seen that this couldn't be further from the truth. Just as I believe that the natural world can reveal glimpses of heaven, I also believe that animals can be messengers of the divine, teaching us through their companionship and compassion what heaven is really like. Like us, animals can share and give love and like us they have souls, souls that survive after death. They are made of the same energy that humans are and in my mind there is no reason why they may not survive in the same way.

Love in whatever shape or form it takes is always stronger than death, as this next story from Ashanti shows.

Put to sleep

Life felt empty when my gorgeous yellow Labrador dog died. Charles had been my best friend for fifteen years. My dad ran him over by accident. He survived the accident but the surgery and aftercare were just too expensive and he might not have pulled through so we had to make the heartbreaking decision to have him put to sleep. I felt so guilty, even though I knew I had no other option. I was also very angry with my dad because when he drove out that morning he was on his mobile phone and wasn't looking around him as much as he should have been.

Charles always felt more like a human than a dog to me; that's why I gave him such a grown-up, non-doggy name. He had such life and such personality. I loved him so much and I know he loved me. I had trained and loved him every day and couldn't stop crying. Everything reminded me of him. He was the best thing in my life and then he was gone. I had never felt so empty or so alienated from my dad.

And then I had two incredible experiences which have convinced me he is still watching over me. The first happened after a meal out with my dad. Dad was clearly trying to build bridges with me, but I was still blaming him for Charles's death. He had apologized many times over but I wasn't listening and we ate much of our meal in silence. I knew I was hurting my dad because he loved me very much, but in a way I wanted him to hurt as I was hurting too. That probably doesn't make sense but it was how I felt at the time. We finished the meal and there was quite a lot of meat left over. The waiter came over and asked us if we would like a doggie bag for our dog. I told him that we didn't have a dog. The waiter looked surprised and told us that he had been outside smoking when we arrived and had seen us getting out of the car and there was a yellow dog sitting in the back. When we had gone inside the dog had made him laugh because he got up and sat in the driver's seat of the car and looked as if he was going to drive off with his paws on the steering wheel.

184

The waiter had no reason to make any of this up as I didn't know him and he didn't know us. The only possible conclusion is that he had seen Charles in spirit and Charles was sending me a message by sitting in the driver's seat – Dad's seat. He wanted me to forgive Dad because he clearly had forgiven him.

The second was a really vivid dream. In my dream I was walking outside, and it was a nice, sunny day. Charles ran up to me and demanded to be thrown his ball as he always did. I happily obliged and we hung around like old times, playing and walking in the sunshine. Suddenly – he ran away from me and started to leave. I followed him, trying to catch up, but he was too fast for me. He turned around and gave me one last look and then disappeared. This was the last time I would ever see him. He hasn't haunted my dreams since, nor have I had any other odd experiences. But I feel as if this was his spirit coming to give me one last goodbye.

The appropriately named Angel also believes her cat returned for one last goodbye:

Burning bright

Tiger was my baby. She was most the most stunningly beautiful Persian cross you can imagine. She also had the loudest purr you ever heard – now I know why they call them purrsians – and I lived with Tiger and loved her every second of the five years we spent together until she got very ill and needed to be put to sleep.

One morning I was sitting in my chair drinking my tea and watching breakfast TV when I felt something jump on the back of the sofa and brush past my neck. Then I felt something kneading my left shoulder. Tiger always used to do that when she was alive. It was part of our morning ritual. I also felt warmth, happiness and light all around me, I wasn't daydreaming or dreaming. I didn't imagine it. Tiger came back for one last goodbye.

Pat is in no doubt that her beloved pets returned to let her know they were still there.

Still there

When our dog Bobbie passed away, it was so very sad — this dog was more like a human and gave such love to us. One day soon after, my daughter and I were sitting in the conservatory when we both looked at each other and said at the same time, 'I can smell Bobbie.' I feel sure that he was visiting us and letting us know that he was still here.

A few years ago we started feeding a stray cat — an unkempt little thing with an injured paw and only two teeth left in her mouth. It took a few months of being patient but at last she trusted us and when winter came she came into the house. We had lots of visits to the vet with one problem and another, and she went through many operations for cancer. She passed away last year. She loved to sit on my lap of an evening and curl up and go to sleep there for hours. After she died I was lying on the settee while my husband was making a cup of tea in the kitchen, and I saw her jump onto my lap. She must still be with us and this is where she wanted to be. I feel sure that she came to visit us, perhaps in the evening time so that she could curl up on my lap like she used to.

Ashanti, Angel and Pat are not alone in their experiences. Many people who have lost beloved pets are convinced that their animals come back in spirit to reassure them. Having researched spirits of humans and animals I have no hesitation in stating that animal spirits are just as common as the ghosts of humans. I've read hundreds of reports from people who say they have smelled, sensed, heard or felt the spirit of their recently departed pets, and have also had experience of this phenomenon myself. After the death of my beloved cat Crystal I could often feel her jumping on my bed at night, just as she always used to, and in the morning for several months after she died I would see an imprint of her body on the bed.

Some people report repeated visits from their pets in spirit but most of the encounters tend to happen only once, as if the animal has returned to say one last goodbye. All the people I spoke to who had experienced this phenomenon told me that the meeting, however brief, gave them great comfort, and helped them overcome feelings of guilt, allowing them to move forward with their lives. This doesn't surprise me. Like angels, the love that our pets have for us is unquestioning, unconditional and constant. They can offer us comfort and courage when we need it and calm us with their presence. As I've said repeatedly in this book, angels come in all shapes and sizes, and for people who feel a strong spiritual connection with their pets in both this life and the next, there is no doubt that some angels have more than two legs.

So far, we've seen that nature and animals can offer us life-changing glimpses of the divine, but I'd like to go on now to yet another powerful, but often unrecognized, way that angels can reveal themselves and change lives in the process, and that is through the magic of coincidences.

The magic of coincidences

We've all experienced them – a friend calls just as we are thinking of him or her, or a romantic partner has the same birthday we do or we hear a song that speaks directly to our hearts. Some coincidences are small and seemingly inconsequential, but others have the potential to change lives – saving them or turning them around – because they can reassure us that we are on the right path and being guided in the direction we need to go.

The dictionary defines coincidences as 'striking chance occurrences', but when they happen they always feel like so much more than mere chance. For me, coincidences are nothing short of mini-miracles, because they make us feel protected and guided and give witness to a higher power. When they happen even sceptics may find themselves wondering what is behind it all. Sure, it is easy to dismiss the magic as chance or luck, but if we could stop doubting and simply open our minds to the possibility that something magnificent might be in tune with us when coincidences happen, our lives can be transformed.

Coincidences or synchronicity have certainly been important in shaping my life. I often look back and with the benefit of age and hindsight think how the pieces of my life have all fitted together like a puzzle. At the time I may have wondered why an experience happened, but I can see now that every experience

I have had in my life, every person I have met, everything that has happened to me, has brought me to the place I am now in my life. It will be the same for you.

Think about the people who are in your life right now and the way coincidences, chance encounters or events have brought you together. This right-time, right-place phenomenon happens so many times I don't even call it coincidence any more, I call it life in spirit. Think about situations in your past that just seemed to work out. Think about all the coincidences out there waiting for you to encounter them. Over the years I've learned that the more I become aware of coincidences and the more I express appreciation for them the more likely I am to encounter them in my life. Feelings of gratitude have a truly awesome power in the world of spirit and invite the magic of coincidences, the magic of angels into your life.

I believe that in coincidences the angels are calling out to us. And to understand what they are trying to say, all we need to do is listen to them, trust them and thank them. Like countless other people who have been encouraged, inspired, saved or comforted by the miracle of coincidences, Claudia is in no doubt that a higher power was speaking to her.

Beyond coincidence

I have just finished reading your book and felt I had to share my own experience with you.

When I was seventeen years old, my granddad passed away unexpectedly, and the whole family was utterly devastated, especially my mum, who was my granddad's youngest child. I vowed to name my first son Peter in memory of him, even though I had no intention of having any children until I was a lot older. Two years after he died, my mum was still affected by his death, couldn't cope and was a shadow of her former self. Naturally, this was upsetting and I prayed every night that my mum would go back to her old self and be happy again. One night, I had a vivid dream in which my granddad told me I was going to have a very special baby, and the baby was going to make us all happy again. I remember feeling very happy when I woke up, but thinking it couldn't be right as I didn't have a boyfriend and was thinking of applying to college.

A year after that, I applied to college, was accepted and enjoyed my course and making new friends. My friends on the course were arranging for a get-together at one girl's house for us all to get to know each other better, and so the night of the party came and there was lots of fun, laughter and a good atmosphere. We decided to go to a club and carry on the night, and at the last minute, as we were leaving, I decided to leave my coat there as it was new and I didn't want to lose it! We had a great night, and two of my friends decided to leave to get a taxi home.

Suddenly I remembered my coat, and my friends agreed to go the short walk with me so I could get it. This was in the exact opposite direction to where we were getting the taxi. On our way there, we met three guys who said they had been in the same club as us, so they walked with us, just chatting about what a good night it had been. I was drawn to one of them, Jack — he was quiet, and looked very familiar but I couldn't put my finger on it. We got chatting, and something just clicked with us. Almost as if I was 'home' at last. He then told me he was a single parent, and he had a little boy called Peter! Also, Peter had Down's syndrome, and Jack was very much the proud father, showing me pictures on his mobile and speaking sadly about Peter's mother not accepting his condition and cutting all ties with him. We met a couple more times before I met Peter, and when I did, he was only seven months old but he gave me such a deep look that I felt my heart swelling and the hairs on the back of my neck stood up. I fell in love with Peter instantly and knew this was the baby my granddad meant.

My mum now says that my granddad sent little Peter to heal us, as our lives are once again full of joy, laughter and lots of fun. Five years on, Jack and I are still so happy together and Peter is our very own little angel. He was definitely heaven-sent, and I am convinced that my granddad is our angel working to make us happy.

I'm sorry that this is such a long email, but I felt I just had to share my story. I have always believed in angels, as the first time I saw one was when I nearly died from meningitis when I was five. I believe there are no such things as coincidences, only our angels working together to enrich our life experiences.

Angels can send their life-changing messages in many different ways, and it's entirely possible that they have already been speaking to you on many occasions without you even realizing it. Whatever form these messages take they will most typically be unique and meaningful for the person involved, as is often the case for coincidences, but there are some signs that seem to occur time and time again – signs that are easily identified as messages from the angels. Perhaps one of the most common, and one that I certainly receive the highest number of emails about, are white feathers. It's hard to believe that something as small and apparently trivial as a white feather can have such a huge impact on a person's life, but to those who believe, like Ava whose story is below, the effect is nothing short of marvellous.

Tiny white feathers

In 2005 I was diagnosed with bowel cancer. I was very scared and upset and prayed to my angels to send me some sign that they hadn't forgotten me. Soon after, for about two weeks before my operation when I was at my most vulnerable, I began to notice tiny white feathers in many unusual places, tucked into my jumper or randomly landing on my lap. I don't have any explanation for these feathers as I don't have feather pillows or duvets in my house. The operation went well and to date I have been absolutely fine.

The discovery of some white feathers was a big comfort to Bronte.

Flying free

When my pet budgie died I was surprised how upset it made me. I'd had him for nearly five years and he always lifted my spirits. I missed him so much but couldn't really tell any of my friends and family – I mean, he was just a budgie. They didn't understand that he was more than that to me. Sometimes I would come home and be convinced that he was still tweeting in his cage. It just didn't seem real that he had died and I so longed to think of him flying high and flying free after his death. I got the sign I had been hoping for about a month after his death when I found a pair of the most astonishingly pure white feathers on his grave in the garden. People may say I'm crazy but in my heart I believe this was his way of letting me know he was flying free.

And Maria believes that finding white feathers in random places is a sign that she is being watched over by her guardian angel.

Watched over

I bought your book a few months after I started finding white feathers in the most random places and I wanted to know what the meaning was. I now have hope that my feathers will bring me happiness, as I had always hoped they might be from my guardian angel. Last night I went downstairs and this white feather came floating down from out of nowhere. I don't have any feather dusters or pillows or cushions, so I know it is a sign that I'm being watched over.

Michael is in no doubt that finding white feathers is a sign from his departed wife that she is still around, because it was his wife who taught him the meaning of white feathers.

New meaning

I lost my wife just before our wedding anniversary and it was and is a bitter blow. My kids were a huge support and continue to take care of me, but the single most important thing in my coping strategy has been a large white feather. I never believed in angels or any of that stuff, but my wife did and before she died she promised to send me a white feather to let me know she hadn't gone far away. On our wedding anniversary I woke up and for a moment it felt as if my wife was sleeping beside me with her arm over my chest. I lay there savouring the moment but then when I realized she wasn't there the sadness returned. I got up and when I did I found that a long white feather was stuck to my chest. I knew it was the sign my wife had promised to send me. I knew she was still around.

In addition to feathers, other commonly recognized angel signs are coins that turn up in unusual places, lights flickering, doorbells ringing with no one there, clocks stopping at significant times, phones ringing with no one on the line and, as you'll see in Cheryl's lovely story below, lost items that have great personal meaning somehow turning up at just the right time.

Lost and found

My gran and granddad bought me a silver bracelet for Christmas 2001. I loved it. My granddad surprisingly passed away on 2 February 2002 from a cancer we had only just found out he had! From the day of his death I vowed I would never take the bracelet off and I didn't. I knew it was risky wearing it to my job as a nursery nurse but I loved it so much.

One October day at work I realized my bracelet was missing. I had everyone searching everywhere but to no avail. I even looked on the way home and turned my house upside down but it was nowhere to be found! I looked every day at work in the hope of finding it but it was useless. I cried and I prayed.

One Monday a couple of weeks later I was changing a child's nappy, I looked in her bag for some cream but couldn't find any so tipped the bag out . . . there at the bottom of her nappy bag caught in the netting was my bracelet. Was it just luck her mum hadn't emptied the bag at the weekend and found it or did an angel or my granddad keep it safe for me to find? I like to think my granddad saw how much it meant to me and sent it back for me.

Another commonly recognized angel calling card is hearing songs that 'just happen' to be playing at the right time. Dawn describes the phenomenon.

Simply the best

When my husband went to work on Monday he heard on the radio 'Build Me Up Buttercup', which was one of the songs played at my sister's funeral. The next day he heard on the radio 'We Are Family', a song I often sang with my sister. The next day he told me he had heard 'Maggie May' – my sister was called Maggie – and that same evening we were sitting talking about work, family and so on and we both saw an orb of light flash past us. Later my husband and I were talking in bed when he jokingly said he couldn't wait to see if any more significant songs came on the radio the next day. I said, 'If you hear "Simply the Best" or "More Than Words" then my sister is definitely with you.' He looked at me and said both of the songs had been on the radio that day but he hadn't connected them to anything. I said, 'Don't you remember they were the other two songs played at Maggie's funeral?' We were both blown away! I truly believe my sister has been around my husband this week and it is her way of reaching out to me.

Another sign that many people write to me about is a beautiful fragrance, typically floral, that has no apparent source.

Belinda describes her experience below:

Divine waiting room

I had a strange but wonderful thing happen to me in 2005. One night I went to bed and there was the most beautiful smell in my room. When my husband came in he said, 'Wow, I love your new perfume,' but I wasn't wearing any. The smell stayed with me all night and then from time to time over the next few days I would smell it just for a moment or two.

About a week later I found out I had breast cancer. The cancer wasn't a nice one. It spread and after lots of operations I ended up having my breast removed. Now I had always said that if that happened to me I would end my life. I just knew I would never be able to live with that. But instead of feeling depressed I was on top of the world. It was one of the most amazing times in my life. I just felt alive and happy. Once all the surgery was over and I was back on my feet, my lovely smell left and I was back in my body. Well, that's what it felt like, like I had been taken out of my body while someone else dealt with the cancer. Then when it was over I was put back. I've always said I waited in God's waiting room. I was calm, happy and I didn't cry, not once. I just went with it, which is not me – everyone thought I would go to pieces but I didn't. I had invisible help. I live my life on pure faith now. I trust and am full to the brim with love and always have time for others, even if it is to chat to someone who is lonely. I believe I am here for a reason. I'm not religious at all but I do trust my god and after reading your book I ask my angels to show me signs and they always do.

Belinda's story is inspiring for me and I hope it will inspire you too. Scent is also a theme in Jacqueline's story.

Not of this world

My experience happened in 1999, a few days before my father passed away. I was on my own in the house as my son was away on a school trip and I went to bed around ten p.m. and fell asleep shortly after.

A little later I woke up and it felt as if something had woken me as I'm sure I felt a tickle on my cheek. I looked at the clock and saw that it was eleven-twenty-five, so I hadn't been asleep long. I sat up in bed a little bothered that I had to try and get back to sleep again and it was then that I smelled very strong, flowery perfume.

I lifted the duvet closer to see if I'd spilled anything on it and then, as my bed was next to the window, looked all along the windowsill to find out where the smell was coming from. It was a sweet smell and I got out of bed to go to the bathroom, expecting to still smell it all around the room. However, it was only around the bed and when I got back into bed I felt a little afraid and asked out loud for whatever was happening to stop as I was very anxious.

I managed to get back to sleep and slept very well. The following day I went to three different florists to find if the smell from any of the flowers matched the smell that had been in my room. I couldn't find it and can only wonder if perhaps I was visited by an angel or perhaps a relative that had passed over to let me know that Dad was all right and I would be all right.

From reading your book you mention perfume as one of the ways in which an angel makes contact, so I draw comfort from this.

Both music and scent feature in Anne's story:

Not really you

The day of my mother's funeral was a long tiring day; not all sad as we had arranged a lovely service and many family members were present. One of the pieces of music I chose to be played was Brahms' Lullaby, as my mother used to sing it to any little ones in the family. My husband had gone home in a different car early as he works nights, and I drove home alone from my sister's house. The drive takes about an hour and a half. I drove to the main road, went round the roundabout and was just wondering if the actual cremation of my mother's body had taken place — not a very pleasant thought! — and I said aloud, 'But don't worry, Mummy, because that's not really you!' and switched the radio on to distract myself. It was tuned to Classic FM and immediately the music of Brahms' Lullaby started, from the beginning. I was stunned. I have never heard it played on Classic FM before or since. I didn't think it was just a coincidence, but felt it was a definite message from my mother.

A road had been closed and I had to go another way, adding another half an hour onto the journey. I was so tired and again said aloud (although I don't normally talk aloud to myself in the car!) 'I'm so tired!' and immediately I could smell a sweet perfume, perhaps lavender. It was so strong that I was looking round the car to see what it could be and wondering whether I had brought any flowers back with me, even though I knew I hadn't. It lasted only a very short time and later I realized that it was probably linked to my mother. On the day she died, I brought some lavender from home and put three sprigs on her pillow next to her dead body – as I had done when my father died.

I have never experienced anything like the music and the scent before or since.

As well as heavenly music and scent you may also get a feeling that someone is gently touching you or kissing. It's a very gentle, subtle and tender touch, just to let you know that your angels are there caring for you. An unexpected sense of emotional wellbeing, this feeling of being loved and cared for, is also the work of your guardian angel.

Other people have written to tell me that they find themselves drawn for no particular reason to a newspaper they never usually buy or a kind of magazine or book they normally wouldn't be interested in and then when they read it they find the answers or reassurance they have been seeking. Some tell me they experience the same when they switch on the radio, TV or go online, or see messages on cars or billboards that speak volumes to them. There may also be the reappearance of a certain number at significant times, most commonly the number 11. High-pitched ringing in the ear that stays for a short time, or the feeling that someone is standing behind you, are other common angel calling cards. And, as mentioned earlier in the book, some people hear the clear, calm voice of an angel from within them, and there is a sudden realization or a moment of truth when everything in their life makes sense.

If you experience any of these sensations my advice is to welcome them as opportunities to connect with your guardian angel. If you can, close your eyes and for a few moments thank your guardian angel for being close by. The angels are always there trying to reassure you and will leave their calling cards in unique ways that make sense only to you.

If you open your heart to them you really can find angels anywhere and everywhere. There is nothing complicated or out of reach about your angels. You can find them anywhere from rainbows and clouds to numbers and music, from sunlight to moonlight, from kind words to every positive thought and act of generosity. Angels can be found in every atom of creation. They are part of the inter-connection between this world and the next. As Maria says in her story below, to experience the wonder and the comfort that your angels can bring, all you need to do is believe.

Just believe

I want to congratulate you for the book *An Angel Healed Me*. I finished reading it last week and I was really excited to find that I had encountered signs more often as I thought I had. The strange thing is, once I entered the bookshop I was walking straight in its direction and I wasn't even aware of that. I didn't read anything but the title but for some reason I knew I had to buy it.

Since reading your book many things have happened to me: I found two white feathers, I started to get over my past and while I was reading at the end of your book about signs that people get from angels I felt them at exact moment I read about them, one after another, the message clearly saying, 'I'm here!'

But one of the most important things that happened was that I remembered one time when I escaped death by a few seconds. I was about five or six at the time, and I went to the beach with my mum and there was this 'banana ride'. It was like an inflatable boat and my friend and I wanted to climb on it. There were other people too and when I did manage to climb on, I fell off. At first it wasn't such a big deal as the water wasn't deep, less than half a metre, but after that a wave came and pulled the boat on top of me. It was so unexpected I didn't have time to get any air. Sure, it didn't seem such a big deal as it was floating, but more and more people got on it and as it was so close to the beach I could have easily got squashed without anyone knowing. I didn't have any air in my lungs and they were literally burning. I was also scared my tummy and legs would get scratched by the sea shells at the bottom. I wasn't a good swimmer either and even though I'd managed to get to the other side another wave could come and push me under the water again. I was trapped!

I thought that was it, I was either going to get squashed by the inflatable boat and all the people on it, or drown or altogether! I couldn't escape!

Just then I heard a voice in my head, calm but full of confidence: 'You are going to live! It's not your time! SWIM! You have to get to the other side! You're strong! You can do it! Nearly there! Swim!'

To my amazement I did manage to get to the other side without a scratch. After that I was too happy to be alive to think that my guardian angel had been speaking to me, even though I did wonder how I had survived and what I had heard. But now all these years later I finally know. I started crying when I realized it and I couldn't stop, my heart was full of so much warmth and love. I've been missing so much.

It was also around that time that I woke up one morning and found that there was water condensed on my window but forming an angel shape in the middle. On its right, where my bed is, it looked like there was someone next to the angel. I quickly realized that it was me and it was another sign to make me aware that there is something that is watching over me.

It's so amazing that all I needed to do was to believe and that's what your book made me do. I told my friend about all this and she said, 'You are so lucky! Your guardian angel is watching over you . . .' but I replied, 'You have one too, everyone does. All you have to do is believe!' as I now know that from my own experience.

Angel signs, or calling cards, are deeply personal ways for our angels to reveal themselves to us. The meaning is typically clear only to the person experiencing them, because they speak directly to the person's heart, and their heart alone. That's why these angel signs tend to be subtle, or recognized only with the benefit of hindsight. There is nothing subtle, however, in the way angels reveal themselves in the next couple of stories. That's because all the people involved believe they actually met an angel. Let's begin with Antonia's experience.

Special drink

When my six-month-old daughter Mona first got a bout of diarrhoea, I didn't think much about it. I thought she was just teething. My other three children had all experienced something similar. I was a bit concerned because she was very cranky but as I said I didn't think too much about it. When you get to your fourth child you are much more laid-back than you ever thought you might be when you have your first one.

Mona fell asleep around seven and around seven-thirty the doorbell rang. It was a woman who told me she was selling cleaning products and that her name was Lily. I just wasn't in the mood so told her quite firmly — thank you, but no thank you. Just before I closed the door the woman told me she had been passing by and heard a baby crying. I don't know why but I told her that Mona had an upset stomach. The woman said she didn't want to interfere but my baby's life might be in danger. I was stunned. I didn't know diarrhoea could be dangerous. She told me to give Mona a special drink to prevent her body dehydrating. She said I needed to mix the drink with a little salt and sugar.

There was something so authoritative about this lady that I didn't hesitate to follow her advice. I spoon-fed my baby the drink after every loose motion and by midnight she was getting her strength back. The next morning I told both my neighbours about the special drink and the saleswoman and asked them if she had called round to see them too. Both were in at the time but neither had had a call from her. What's also extraordinary about this is that the lady said she heard a baby crying when she was passing, but Mona had been asleep for a good half an hour before the doorbell rang. Also, I contacted the cleaning company the lady said she worked for and there was no record of anyone working for them with the name of Lily.

There are just too many things that I can't explain about that lady. I believe she was Mona's guardian angel and mine too – I would never have forgiven myself if something had happened to Mona because I didn't take her condition seriously enough.

You've probably heard stories about mysterious strangers who seem to appear at the right time to lend assistance to a person in need and then vanish afterwards. These strangers are often called 'angels' and I'm aware that for many people stories like this can be explained logically. Perhaps the woman was just a kind person who came along at the right time to give advice and lend a helping hand. Yet, there is something that doesn't add up about many stories like the one sent to me by Antonia. For example, why couldn't she trace the woman through her company and why did the woman say she heard a baby crying when the house was silent when she rang the doorbell? If the lady was an angel no explanation is required. If she wasn't, perhaps the angels led her to Antonia's door. No matter the explanation, whether human or divine, that lady will always be an angel in Antonia's eyes, just as a passing stranger will always be an angel to the people involved in this next story.

Our guardian angel

Benjamin Nelson-West was with his mother Adrianna on a Piccadilly Line platform at Acton Underground station in west London when the accident happened on 31 July 2009. A train pulled in and Adrianna got in. Then she started screaming. Benjamin had lost his footing and was stuck in the gap between train and platform. The train doors were starting to close and at that moment Tochukwu Mokah, an engineer from Nigeria who was waiting for another train, lay down on the platform, put his hands in the gap and pulled the child to safety. After he had passed the boy to his mother, the train pulled out with Mr Mokah still on the platform and Mrs Nelson-West and her son on the train. Everything happened so fast, she didn't even get a chance to say thank you. It took a while to track him down but eventually Mrs Nelson-West was reunited with and could express her heartfelt gratitude to her son's 'guardian angel'.

This story was reported in the media at the time and I'm placing it here because it is a fantastic reminder that in the right place and at the right time we all have the potential to be guardian angels. We can all be guided by the angel inside us and by so doing bring a glimpse of heaven on earth to others.

June, whose experience is below, might agree since she cannot explain where the miraculous vision and strength came from that saved her grandchild's life.

Change of opinion

I'm a frail seventy-seven-year-old lady and ever since I was diagnosed with diabetes I've been short on energy and strength. I
certainly wouldn't describe myself as strong. I've changed my opinion
about myself though and I think my children and husband have too.
It happened two years ago when I was looking after my two-year-old
grandson. I'd felt odd all afternoon and after I'd put him to bed I felt
even worse. I decided to go to bed too. When I was in bed I felt so
sick and shaky that I decided to call 999 but I couldn't even use my
fingers to dial.

All I could think about was my grandson and somehow I staggered
into his bedroom, picked him up and got him outside the house. I
think passers-by must have thought I'd had a stroke because they
called for an ambulance. When the paramedics arrived I started to
recover. I told them I didn't need to go to hospital but they insisted
on checking me out. We went into my house and it was then that the
paramedics realized something was very wrong because they started
to feel weak, dizzy and ill too. They suspected carbon-monoxide
poisoning and they were proved right. The build-up of carbon monox-
ide was caused by a blocked flue from the gas central heating boiler.

If I'd stayed in that house any longer I'd have died and so would
my precious grandson. I don't know where I got the strength from
to pull him out but I think it came from above. I also think my story
shows that you can surprise everyone, including yourself, at any age.

Ruby also has no idea where the uplifting words came from that
turned a person's life around.

Speaking from the heart

I was on a train to London and a woman sat down next to me. I could tell that she was troubled. I didn't say anything because I'm not really the chatty type but throughout the journey I couldn't stop thinking about her. She reminded me strongly of the woman I was just after I found out my husband had had an affair. Back then I had felt unhappy and betrayed but I tried to soldier on with a brave face because I believed marriage was for life.

When the train drew into Paddington I made eye contact with the woman and smiled. She smiled back weakly and before I knew it I said something that my grandma told me when I was dealing with my marriage breakdown: 'If it doesn't make you happy, let it go.' These simple words changed my life for the better because they helped me see that I wasn't happy and probably never would be with my husband, and it was time for us both to call it a day.

Now, I don't know where these words came from and I surprised myself when I spoke them. I felt embarrassed and tried to get out of the train fast but the woman reached out to me and said, 'Thank you. How did you know?'

We entered into a short conversation as we walked down the platform together. Turns out I had been right. She wasn't married but she was having an affair with a married man. She kept hoping he would leave his wife for her but he never did. She told me that I must be psychic because I knew what she was going through. She told me that this was the sign she was looking for and she was going to end the affair and move forward with her life.

I'm not psychic. I just spoke from my heart. I don't know where those words came from or how I got the courage to just say them like that to a complete stranger, but it was a wonderful feeling to watch that woman walk away with a smile on her face.

Perhaps, like June and Ruby, we can all do the work of angels on earth from time to time by offering simple words of heart-felt empathy, love and kindness that may help others see a way forward, or glimpse a piece of heaven on earth. Perhaps we can all discover within ourselves feelings of love, compassion, strength, beauty, and courage that not only light up our lives, but the lives of all those lucky enough to cross our path.

Remember, if you can change one person you can change the world.

Why not, in the words of Mahatma Gandhi, begin with yourself and become the change you want to see in the world.

CHAPTER 7

Beyond the Veil

For death begins with life's first breath
And life begins at touch of death.

John Oxenham

Death is something we must all face. None of us, however rich, clever or famous, can escape it. Death unites us all. Not surprisingly, the finality of death, coupled with doubt or uncertainty about the afterlife, is a source of great fear and anxiety for many of us.

I think one of the reasons why so many of us fear death is because it is the great unknown. I was certainly terrified about it in my youth, but the countless stories I have read over the years about near-death experiences and visions of the afterlife, as well as reunions with loved ones in spirit, has taken some of the sting out of death for me. I have come to understand that the fear we have is simply fear of facing the greatest change of all, fear of leaving our physical body behind and beginning a new life in spirit. It doesn't have to be that way, though, if we could regard death not as the end, but as a wonderful new beginning.

Regrettably, society surrounds the event of death with secrecy, and few of us are really prepared for it. We find it hard to talk about death, or even think about it, but the reality of angels on earth proves that death is not the end. It is just another phase in your existence and so much awaits you in the afterlife. If you think about it, you start dying the moment you are born and when you go to sleep at night your consciousness leaves your body and travels to the world of spirit. In the morning you may recall some of the dreams you had, but in a sense it doesn't really matter whether you remember or understand your dreams or not, it just shows that every day of your life you are dying and living again whether you realize it or not.

I hope reading the stories in this the final chapter about remarkable people who have glimpsed life beyond the veil will show you that physical death is not to be feared. It is just another natural process, and in this life and the next it is hate, fear, anger and guilt that kill rather than death itself. Death is despair of the heart and emptiness of the soul. Therefore, for those living in spirit there is no death as such, only darkness when there is no light. For in the light there is no death, only everlasting goodness and love.

Above all, I hope what you read here will go some way to replacing any fear or uncertainty you may have about death and passing over to the other side with a newfound sense of hope and peace.

What is death?

To understand death, we first need to understand life.

In recent decades scientists have tried to pinpoint the differences between non-living organisms and living organisms. They found two key differences – cell walls and chromosomes that enable them to replicate or reproduce themselves. So they tried to create artificial life forms with cell walls and transplanted chromosomes. They gave these artificial life forms electric shocks, but they were still not alive, in the sense that they did not have the intelligence, feelings and spirit that define our understanding of life. The only conclusion that could be drawn is that there is something invisible or unseen that makes organisms live.

I call this invisible life force 'spirit'.

What we can learn from unsuccessful scientific attempts to create intelligent life is that the idea that death is the end of our existence is irrational. Your heart may stop beating and your physical body fade away, but the invisible part of you remains. In this way, death is not the end of everything, just spirit leaving your body. In short, the essence of you – your spirit – survives.

If you've ever said goodbye to the body of a loved one, deep down you may already know this to be true. I was in my late teens when I saw a dead body for the first time. I was working in an old people's home as a care assistant at the time. Whenever a resident died, I remember thinking their body looked like clothes that weren't being worn any more. The essence of the person had gone. It wasn't them lying on the bed or in the coffin. That was one of the main reasons I didn't want to see my mum's body when she died. I knew she wasn't there any more. I sensed her presence far more whenever I thought or dreamed about her. To me, she still felt alive, somewhere.

The idea that a loved one hasn't died but lives on in spirit is a theme I have found over and over again in many of the stories sent to me over the years. In almost every case something unexpected or astonishing happens, leaving the person with a powerful belief that their loved one is 'alive' in spirit and watching over them.

Before we begin, I just want to bring some clarity here in my use of the terms 'angel' and 'spirit'. You may already have noticed that I use the terms interchangeably, even though in the strictest sense there are differences, in that angels are invisible spiritual beings who have never lived on earth. The reason I use the terms interchangeably is because I believe that our angels can choose to manifest their presence and their message of hope and comfort through the spirits of departed loved one.

This first inspiring story comes from Lesley.

Incredible things

Since my beloved dad's passing on 1 January 2010, a few incredible things have happened and I want to share them with you.

Two and a half years before, Dad was told he had a brain tumour. He fought long and hard. He went on to have weeks of radiotherapy and eventually was told that he was in remission. Even though tears of joy flowed and there was temporary relief he was never fully healthy again and suffered from sporadic mini-seizures. Then in September last year we heard the devastating news that the tumour was back and very aggressive. Dad started having trouble walking and talking. Things went from worse to worse and in October he was admitted to hospital, then a nursing home and finally a hospice where the angels came and took him away.

In the final days I was with him along with my mum and my twenty-five-year-old daughter who was pregnant at the time. We are such a close family. Dad was everything to us all. When he died my heart was broken. I was angry at everyone, even my mum. I could not bear the way she gave away all his belongings. I looked at men his age walking around and resented that they were alive and Dad wasn't.

My daughter stayed at my flat for a few days after Dad died. She was heartbroken too and her husband was working a lot and I didn't want her to be alone. I let her sleep in the bed and I had the settee and this is when I started to have strange experiences. I had gone to sleep but I woke to the sound of a low-flying aircraft, but not outside – inside my head. Then I saw Dad rush past me calling out my name. I couldn't move, even though I wanted to.

A week later I was half asleep and half awake but fully aware when I heard the sound of flapping wings, like a bird. It was right against my ear. Again I couldn't move, even though I wanted too. My heart raced but I wasn't scared. This has happened once more, when I also saw a flash of light and felt a mild electrical vibration pass through my body. Also, ever since Dad died, every day I have had a feeling that I can only describe as like walking through a cobweb, or a gentle tickling on my face or in my hair.

Perhaps the most incredible thing that happened was a couple of months ago when this calm, clear voice came into my head to tell me my daughter would have her baby on 22 March. I told my daughter and the day was about three weeks before her due date. Her labour began on 21 March and on 22 March at nine-forty-seven her beautiful baby boy Jacob John was born. I was with her at the birth and as he was coming into the world she was crying and holding my hand with her husband on the other side. I was crying too and we both knew who we were thinking of. All of a sudden it felt like someone had draped a cloak of warmth around my shoulders. It was a very unreal but wonderful feeling and once again it convinced me that my dad is always close by.

Jan also believes that her departed father is never far away.

The pact

As a teenager I made a pact with my father, who did not believe in the world of spirit. Whoever died first would come back to confirm that there is life after death. My father humoured me and, laughing, said he would no doubt die before me but we shook hands.

Many years later I married and had a daughter. My daughter was still very young when I had secondary infertility treatment and the wound (after an operation) went septic. My father had passed away and on my return home I grieved for him. I felt that he had worked so hard all his life instead of enjoying it. It was during one night while I was recuperating at home that I sat up in bed, unable to sleep. I don't know what made me think that my father would come into my bedroom and can only assume it was a way to prepare me for what was to follow.

I felt a presence enter the room and sit on the end of my bed and then I saw my father. We communicated via mental telepathy. There was a bandage on his forehead with a light shining on it and I knew this was to tell me that my wound would heal. I also knew that he is happy now and he communicated that he is studying navigation, which I knew he had loved. He had been in the Second World War and had passed his navigation test with flying colours, something of which he was very proud. All the while my husband slept peacefully beside me.

It was only after I had had the above experience that I remembered our pact. I always knew my father loved me but he was of the generation who had difficulty showing their emotions. This was for me a miracle, showing that the bond of love is never broken, and keeping our pact was an amazing act of love. My father not only came to me, he also appeared to my sister.

This endearing story of love surviving death was sent to me by Marie.

My great-aunt spirit

This happened to me when I was about nine. It is nothing to do with angels, but I have never forgotten it. My great-aunt was my grandma's sister, and she lived with Grandma and Grandpa in their home. When I used to stay with them, I would sleep in her bedroom with her. After she died, I stayed again, in the same bed and room, but of course she was not there with me. I was awake, or at least I believe I was, when my great-aunt came into the room and walked over to the bed. Because she was dead and because I was awake when I should have been asleep, I squeezed my eyes very tightly shut, but I still 'saw' her approach the bed and bend over me. Maybe she tucked me in, I can't remember that bit. I was frightened but comforted at the same time. I could have dreamed this, I suppose, but the memory of it stays with me strongly, despite it being forty-four years ago!

I wrote back to tell Marie that her experience all those years ago had everything to do with angels, as it was still clearly a source of strength and comfort for her.

Pat very kindly sent me her experiences of the afterlife.

I'm all right

My father died very suddenly two years ago. He was a good age, in his eighty-seventh year, but losing him so quickly was quite a shock.

I have had several experiences with dreams and other signs and, as I couldn't settle in my mind, I asked my father to let me know that he was all right and was with my mother, who had passed over some eighteen years previously. Days and weeks went by and every night before I went to sleep I asked him to let me know that he was OK.

Eventually, my father came to me in a dream. I was walking down his road with my two brothers and I saw him in his garden, mowing his lawn. My father loved his garden — it was his pride and joy. I said to my two brothers, 'Look, Father is in the garden, but he can't be, he is dead.' Next, I was in the house, sitting one side of the dining table with my two brothers and my father and my mother were sitting across from us. My father took my hands in his and all he said to me was, 'I'm all right, I'm all right.' I knew then that he was with my mother and that they were happy and together. I stopped worrying about him then because I knew he was all right.

When my mother had passed away, I missed her terribly — she was my best friend, not just my mum. I dreamed that I was in a room with doors all around in a circle. My mother came through one of the doors and put her arms around me. She held me and I started to cry because I missed her so much. Then she told me she had to go back. I tried to follow her through the door but a voice in my head told me that I couldn't go through the door, it wasn't my time.

One night not long after my father had passed away I had this beautiful dream: an angel rose up in front of me — I don't know if it was male or female but it was wearing a purple robe and had large white wings. It wrapped its wings around me and I have never felt such love and peace surround me. I woke up and still had the same beautiful feeling.

Pat mentions comforting dreams in her story, and from my own experience I know that dreams are one of the subtlest and gentlest ways for spirits of departed loved ones to reach out to us and give us messages of support and love from beyond the grave.

Perhaps no dream is more emotionally compelling than a goodbye vision of the recently departed. Jeanne's vivid dream is a lovely example:

Far but near

I am seventeen years old and recently read one of your angel books. I sadly lost my friend recently. We were at a dance competition and she died of a heart attack — it was sudden and unexpected. I knew her from when we was little; we used to go dancing together, and although we grew apart we were still mates. It really hit me when she died, and I do miss her loads. I have memories of us when we were little but sometimes they don't seem enough — she shouldn't have been taken away from us. After she died, I was so upset. She was on my mind constantly, it hurt so much. I got a tattoo of her name, Kelsey, with a star in memory of her.

One night I had a dream that we were at her funeral, but Kelsey was there. We walked together up a flight of stairs and then she sat down. I stood quite far away from her, but she was speaking to me. I could hear her even though we seemed far away. She was surrounded in white light and wearing a gown, and she showed me that she also had a tattoo of my name on her wrist. She told me she loved me, and that she was OK. We were both there showing each other our wrist tattoos. I shouted, 'I love you too!' and that I was glad she was OK.

Psychologists are quick to argue that these kinds of dreams are products of the grieving mind reaching for any kind of temporary relief from the pain of losing someone. While there is logic to this argument, I've come to believe that such dreams are indeed messages of reassurance and love from those who have crossed over. Reading stories about people who believe that they have sensed the spirits of departed loved ones, whether it

218

be through dreams, through signs or coincidences or full-blown encounters, can be extremely comforting because they prove that life doesn't end with death.

Similarly, stories of people who witness something extraordinary when a loved one dies offer us great comfort because they show that when the time comes, when we are perhaps at our most fearful and vulnerable, we are not alone. Jonathon's touching story illustrates this.

Going home

Thirty years ago I had the misfortune to lose both my sons in the space of twenty-four hours. They were involved in a fatal collision. My oldest son, Ron, was driving the car and Mark, my youngest, was in the seat next to him. Mark was the first to die. We didn't tell Ron that Mark had passed because we thought it would limit his chances of recovery, but about an hour and a half before Ron died he told me and my wife that he saw Mark at the bottom of the bed and that Mark had come to take him home.

Losing both your children in such a sudden way is something no parent should ever experience. You don't expect to bury your sons. It feels unnatural to outlive them. At the time I dismissed Ron's vision of Mark as a hallucination, but the older I get the more it comforts me, the more it helps to fill the hole in my heart.

Faith in the power of love was also renewed when Susie witnessed the death of her mother.

A lovely death

I've never believed in angels or in anything really, but that's certainly not the case now and I want to tell you why. I realized there was something more when my mum died following a bout of cancer on 19 June 2002. Two days before she died, she lost consciousness. She looked old, pale and there were lines and marks around her closed eyes. I sat with her and talked to her for many hours during those two days. I wanted to believe that she could hear me, even though the nurses told me she probably couldn't.

On the evening she died I was about to go and get a cup of coffee when something made me stop. I could smell lavender in the room, but there was no source. Then I looked at Mum and her eyes were wide open. She was smiling at me and all the lines and marks of pain and illness had disappeared. She looked beautiful, like the photos I had seen of her as a young woman. Then she looked at the ceiling above her and lifted one arm as if she was about to shake someone's hand. I looked up but couldn't see anything, yet I knew someone was there. I can remember feeling warm from the inside with happiness. Then mum's hand fell onto the bed and she died. It was a lovely death, if death can ever be lovely.

Evidence gathered from first-hand accounts of deathbed scenes is too substantial to be dismissed or ignored. Susie's story stands out because she admitted that before her experience, she was not a woman of faith. Often witnesses observe, as Susie did, a peace and serenity moments before a person's passing. There are also reports of loved ones talking about seeing angels or spirits before they pass over. Becky, a young nurse at the time, believes she actually saw the spirit form of a patient leaving their body. Here's her story.

Night shift

I was on night shift and doing my rounds. I went to check up on one of my patients and it was about four-thirty a.m. When I went into her room, she became wonderfully alert, as some people do very near the end. I sat by her and held her hand and she looked to one side, staring into vacant space. As time went by, it was clear she could see someone there I couldn't. Then her face lit up like a beacon. She was staring and smiling at what was clearly a long-lost friend, her eyes so full of love and serenity that it was hard for me not to be overcome by tears.

Then she closed her eyes and I knew that she had died. I sat for a while in silence, giving the moment the dignity and respect it deserved. When I looked up I saw something rise from her body. It was absolutely beautiful. A whirl of pastel colour, vibrant not only in appearance but also in movement, was leaving her chest area. It was so comforting. Like I said, I was a very young nurse – we are talking 1975 and I'm close to fifty-five now – and at the time I thought that this was probably the body letting off steam or something, but I don't think that now. I believe I saw that old lady's spirit leave her body.

Deathbed visions likes these are far more common than you might think and they have been recorded across nationalities and cultures and religions since the beginning of time. In my opinion, they offer some of the most compelling proof of life after death.

This next story sent by Melanie isn't strictly speaking a death-bed vision, but I want to include it here because once again it shows that we are not alone when the time comes for our final moments on earth.

Special visitor

It happened about four years ago, at the end of June. I was just hanging up the washing in the back garden and had my door open and noticed that my neighbour had her door open too. Half expecting to see her doing the same thing as me, as we sometimes met and had a chat over the fence, I could hear her voice coming from the kitchen. She was talking to someone and though I couldn't see them I could tell the other person was female and I could tell that my neighbour knew her well. There was a closeness to their conversation and I wondered for a moment if it was a relative, which surprised me because my neighbour was housebound and had some regular visitors, but I'd never met any family members before, other than her son and this was wasn't him. But I remember being glad that she had someone with her. I'd seen her husband pop out earlier on.

As I carried on pegging the washing I thought I heard my neighbour ask the other person if she could help her with something and, because my neighbour was quite frail, I wasn't surprised to hear that. I thought the other lady's voice sounded very reassuring and kind as she told her that she was there to help her.

I went back inside and I didn't think it about it again until about an hour later when I saw an ambulance outside the house. I could see my neighbour's car was back, and so I knew her husband was probably there, but I waited discreetly before ringing them to ask if everything was all right, or did they need any help? My neighbour's husband told me that his wife had died while he was out. He had come back and found her lying in the kitchen.

It wasn't till later on that day when I went to see him and I asked if she had had someone with her that he told me she hadn't had any visitors. Anyone coming to see her would need to be arranged so that he could be there to help. There was an autopsy later which confirmed that she had died of natural causes, so he seemed not to worry about my idea other than to tell me that he didn't believe in 'this sort of thing'.

But I had a feeling that my neighbour's visitor had been a special one. Her husband told me she had no relatives, except an aunt she never saw, and when I said that the person she spoke to sounded close 'almost like a sister' he said she had been adopted and had no siblings, as far as they knew. It was a mystery yet every time I thought about them talking, I could hear them so clearly. It sounded like she was with someone she not only knew but had a bond with. And it's brought me comfort since then, even if I couldn't convince her husband. I guess we're not all 'ready' at the same time.

This next story sent to me by Anita also doesn't fit into a specific category, but I'm sharing it with you here because it shows that when a loved one dies our angels are right beside us. It also shows that the sense of comfort and companionship angels can offer us during times of grief or crisis is unparalleled.

Christa

The first incident happened in the summer of 1989 when I was twenty-one and had an eighteen-month-old, William, and I was seven months pregnant with my second baby. One afternoon, while doing the lunch-time dishes, I glanced out of the window and for a split second I saw a little boy of about four or five standing outside, a few feet away from me. He was wearing a white jumper and I was struck by his lovely blond hair. I blinked and he was gone. I put it down to 'seeing things' with being pregnant but a couple of days later when I was out in the garden I looked up from doing the weeding and saw him again. He was wearing the same white jumper and once again I was struck by his mop of golden hair. Then, as before, he disappeared. The next time I saw him from the kitchen window, I told a friend about it and she said it must be my hormones. I told my husband about him too, but he didn't read much into it. I must have seen this little boy about half a dozen times in all.

When I was thirty-eight weeks pregnant I had a takeaway one night and woke up with terrible stomach pains. The pains subsided, and being young and a bit naive, I believed the takeaway hadn't agreed with me and went back to sleep. A few days later, at thirty-nine weeks, I felt what appeared to be labour pains and duly went off to hospital with my packed bag. However, the midwife seemed to be taking a long time to locate a heartbeat and kept winking at me – which I thought was a bit odd. After a while, she told me she couldn't find a heartbeat and it didn't look hopeful. I felt completely numb as the hours passed and doctors came and went doing tests and finally I was told my baby had died and I would have to be induced.

224

It was an awful labour of thirty-plus hours, and I remember watching day turn to night and night into day through the skylight above my head. Eventually the consultant arrived and carried out some procedures – unbeknown to me in my drugged state – and this finally resulted in my little girl, Christa, being born. She was perfect, with a cupid-bow mouth and long slender fingers. Apparently I'd had bleeding around the placenta which had cut off her oxygen supply – resulting in asphyxia – and this was the pains I'd felt a few days earlier.

It wasn't until a couple of weeks after her funeral, while I was standing at the kitchen window, that I remembered my little flaxen-haired visitor, and I'm convinced he was an angel waiting to take Christa to a better place.

My belief in angels has helped me out so many times over the years when I have had difficult times and painful memories to deal with. The sense of comfort and support the angels have given me is tremendous – my only regret is that I didn't start confiding in them years ago.

Then there are those well-documented mystical experiences which offer perhaps the greatest proof, if proof is needed, that there is an afterlife – experiences collectively known as near-death experiences. Regrettably, there isn't time or word count left to give these astonishing experiences the detail and attention they deserve – that will have to wait till another book – but I would like to draw your attention to the incredible work of Dr Elisabeth Kubler-Ross, a psychiatrist whose work with terminally ill people proved to her that there is life after death.

Dr Kubler-Ross's research and writing on the subject of near-death experiences have brought great comfort and hope to millions of people all over the world. Before she began her research, Kubler-Ross admitted that she had no belief in the after-life, but her opinion changed when she began to notice astonishing similarities between thousands of accounts from people all over the world. Near-death experiences or NDEs tend to occur when a person is either clinically dead or in danger of dying and those reported share many similarities. First there is a feeling of calmness and acceptance followed by an intense, pure, bright light that fills the room. The person may feel dissociated from their body in some way, perhaps looking down on it and seeing it, or watching doctors working on it. Many NDE subjects then find themselves in a tunnel with light at the end. Angels and spirit beings may be in the tunnel as they pass through. They may hear the voice of the spirit of a loved one telling them that it is not their time and to go back to their body. There may also be a life review when they see their entire life in flashback.

Reading about near-death experiences and what people on the brink of death have seen, felt, heard and learned can be very beneficial and comforting, because they make it clear that death is not something to be feared and that life doesn't end with death. Elaine's breathtaking story below is a fine example:

The luckiest woman alive

I don't want to go into the details of why I nearly died – as some things are too personal – but I want to tell you what happened. I remember hearing a man saying that he could not find my pulse. I remember feeling surprised because I had never felt more alive. For the first time in my life I was bursting with energy and a sense of purpose. I couldn't hear, see or talk to anyone but it didn't matter. I didn't mind. I just let things go. Next thing I noticed was that I was not alone. I felt like I was where I needed to be and there was a sense of expectation, like the moment before you unwrap a present. There was also no concept of age or time. Everything – my past, present and future – was there with me.

Within moments I experienced an eruption of light from within me and around me. From not seeing or hearing anything, suddenly I could see and hear everything. The light was so bright but my eyes did not burn. I instinctively knew that the light was love, divine love.

I've never believed in God and I've never been religious but I recognized this as sacred. This divine light was directed at me and coming from me. Through the light I had awareness and knowledge. It wasn't like understanding maths or a different language, but understanding the meaning of life. The answers to age-old questions suddenly became obvious. I knew who I was and why I was here and I knew that the purpose of my life was to love. It was like I was remembering things I had always known but had forgotten. It seemed ridiculous that I had not worked things out before.

Then my euphoria was broken and I knew I had to return to my life on earth. I didn't want to but I knew I had to. I was going back and landed back in my body. Later I learned that I had died twice on the operating table. Doctors told me I was the luckiest woman alive. I agree with them, but not in the way they think. I'm not lucky to be alive, because I know that I never died and never will. I'm lucky because the old, confused, purposeless, frightened me died on the operating table and a stronger me was reborn. My experience changed my life for ever.

This is your moment

Many people who have had a near-death experience look back on it in the same way that Elaine did, as a turning point in their lives when fear of death vanishes and is replaced by visions of hope, comfort and, above all, love. They are able to connect with the light of love within themselves, and when they do that they truly begin to live as a spiritual being. They start to see the world through loving eyes and to feel the beauty and joy in all things. In essence, they experience heaven on earth.

But you don't need to have a brush with death, or to see visions of departed loved ones or angels complete with wings and halos, to discover a deeper meaning to your life. As you've seen throughout this book, there are countless opportunities in your everyday life to discover an awareness or realization that you are more than the physical body you live in. Your moment doesn't necessarily have to emerge from a dramatic revelation, personal tragedy or crisis. It may come through an unexpected feeling, a thought, a chance encounter, an answer to a prayer, an insightful dream, or it could come through a sudden surge of joy, a meaningful coincidence or sign that speaks personally and directly to your heart and reacquaints you with everything that is wonderful about living again.

Often it is through simple, unexplained experiences and insights that angels appear within and around us and offer us the opportunity to change our lives for ever. Humble experiences like this one described beautifully and simply by Rose:

Surrounded by warmth

I stood beside my husband's grave. Suddenly, I felt an exhilaration and a deep sense of peace. It came out of nowhere and gave me tremendous comfort. I couldn't see any light, but I felt surrounded by its warmth.

When you are able to connect with the angel within you, as Rose did, you become a beacon of hope and inspiration to others. *You* become the message, because others see a glow of courage, light and love within you and what they see slides into their hearts, reawakening the angel inside them.

So when your opportunity comes you have to make up your mind. You can question what you have experienced, and let it slip away, or you can seize the moment, open your heart to it and let it change your life for ever, and the lives of all those lucky enough to cross your path. You can turn away from the light, or you can bask in the warmth, comfort and joy that is life in spirit.

Whatever path you choose, of one thing you can be certain: your guardian angel will always be watching and waiting for you to choose life.

Afterword: Epiphanies

> *Never fear shadows - they always mean there is a*
> *light shining somewhere.*
>
> Jonathan Santos

In the early stages of this book you may recall that I was reluctant to use the word epiphany because of the strong religious connotations, and angels are not a religion but a spiritual movement that can unite people of all ages, religions and cultures, but now that you have read this far I feel comfortable using it to describe a moment of divine revelation, when life changes for ever.

I pray that reading this book has given you your experience of epiphany. I hope it has helped you look at your life – your past, your present and your future – with feelings of life-changing awe and wonder. I pray that it will have helped you see that angels can be found all around and within you, not just in dramatic encounters or visions of angels, but in everyday feelings, thoughts and experiences.

If you really don't think you have ever had an epiphany, and aren't close to one now, think long and deep.

Perhaps you have had a flash of insight or a surge of elation, of love, or a sense of deep understanding and knowing something you didn't know before, but you've never given that moment enough time or care before because it was too fleeting, just a passing glance and it was gone. Perhaps there have been times in your life when you have surprised yourself by the wise choices you made, the things you said or did, or the courage and dignity you showed. Take your time and look back on your life and remember every uplifting moment when you felt good to be alive.

If you still aren't convinced, and don't remember any sacred moments in your life, then reading about the experiences of others may be the start of something magical for you. The very fact that you are holding this book in your hands is a sure-fire sign that you are already taking your first steps towards finding your moment of recognition, because all you have read here, whether you realize it or not, will help you become more 'aware' of or 'receptive' to the never-ending flow of love that surrounds you and is yours for the taking. You may not be consciously aware of it, but this book has opened the door and you have begun your search for a deeper meaning to life. You are closer than ever before to finding that moment when 'something' can become everything.

Think of this book as your arrow to heaven, a reminder of the constant loving presence of angels in your life from cradle to beyond the grave, and whenever you feel the need of an angel, return to it for strength, guidance, encouragement and inspiration. Return to it to remind yourself that there is no such thing as ordinary, and that every moment of your life can be a moment of possibility, wonder, joy, love, renewal, transformation and magic.

Every day can be the day when angels dip into your heart and into your life and your world is changed – never to be the same again, and nor would you ever wish it to be.

I'd like to close, for now, with some angelic words to inspire and guide you and one of my favourite angel blessings to protect and comfort you.

There are two ways to spread the light and change the world: to be the candle or the mirror that reflects it.

Edith Wharton

Angel blessing

Angels around you, angels beside you, angels within you.
Angels are watching over you when times are good or
    stressed.
Their wings wrap gently around you, whispering you are
    loved and blessed.

About the Author

Theresa Cheung is the author of a variety of books including the *Sunday Times* bestselling: *An Angel Called My Name*, *An Angel on My Shoulder*, and *Angel Babies*. She is also the author of the international bestseller *The Element Encyclopaedia of 20,000 Dreams* and *The Element Encyclopaedia of the Psychic World* and the recent top-10 *Sunday Times* bestseller *An Angel Healed Me*.

Theresa's books have been translated into twenty different languages and her writing has featured in *It's Fate*, *Spirit and Destiny*, *Prediction*, *Red*, and *Prima* magazines, as well as the *Daily Express*, *Daily Mail* and *Sunday Times Style*. In addition, Theresa has worked on books for Derek Acorah, Yvette Fielding, Tony Stockwell and Dr William Bloom. Born into a family of psychics and spiritualists, Theresa has been involved in the research of psychic phenomena for over twenty-five years since gaining a Masters Degree from King's College, Cambridge. She has also been a student at the College of Psychic Studies in London.

Calling all angels

If you have an angel story, experience or insight and wish to share it with Theresa, she would love to hear from you. Please contact her care of Simon and Schuster, 1st Floor, 222 Gray's Inn Road, London, WC1X 8HB or email her direct at: angeltalk710@aol.com

Follow Theresa on the Simon & Schuster website: www.simonandschuster.co.uk